The Authors

Maralene and Miles Wesner are multi-talented teachers and prolific writers. They have published more than 150 Audio-Visual Education aids, and pioneered new reading methods with their Phonics in a Nutshell (1965).

They have written articles, and mission studies for Southern Baptist periodicals. They were in the original group of writers to develop WMU's Big "A" Club material.

They've published several books with Broadman Press: *A Fresh Look at the Gospel* (1983); *You Are What You Choose* (1984); and *How To Be a Saint When You Feel Like a Sinner* (1986) and self-published 30 books by Diversity Press.

They are noted for their no-nonsense style, their clear illustrations, and their willingness to face controversial issues. From the dual perspectives of both academic and religious professions, they seek to be a bridge between the spiritual and the intellectual worlds.

They hold Masters Degrees (MEd) from Oklahoma University plus work toward a Doctorate. Miles also attended Southwestern Baptist Theological Seminary, and served as a high school counselor. He has been the bi-vocational pastor of a small rural church for more than 50 years.

Both Maralene and Miles taught in public school and collages and served as educational consultants. Maralene taught Psychology and Speech for Southeastern Oklahoma State University for 32 years. She was chosen Oklahoma Teacher of the Year in 1975.

They have planned, led tours, and done research in all of the 50 states, Canada, Mexico, Europe, Egypt, Japan, and the Holy Land. In 1985, they were among a small group of Americans who were invited by Dr. Joseph P. Kennedy of the US/China Education Foundation and Bishop Ting, leader of the Three Self Movement, to participate in the First Symposium on the Church in Nanjing, China.

Now, they use their lifetime of varied experiences to write insightful sermons, essays, and books.

Titles by Maralene & Miles Wesner
published by Nurturing Faith

Sermons for Special Days

Life More Abundant

Do You Really Know Jesus?

If Jesus Were Here Today

101 Sparks of Inspiration

When God Can't Answer

Think (Or Else!)

Stumbling to Zion

Sensible Sermons

Finding Truth in the Parables

THE
Unknown
GOD

Maralene & Miles Wesner

© 2024
Published in the United States by Nurturing Faith, Macon, GA.
Nurturing Faith is a book imprint of Good Faith Media (goodfaithmedia.org).
Library of Congress Cataloging-in-Publication Data is available.

ISBN: 978-1-63528-244-3

All rights reserved. Printed in the United States of America.

Scripture quotations are from New Revised Standard Version Bible Updated Edition, copyright © 2021 National Council of the Churches of Christ in the United States of America. Used by permission. All rights reserved worldwide.

Cover photo by Micah Camper on Unsplash.

Contents

Introduction 1
Section 1: We Can Know God by Observing Nature's Design and Beauty 11
Section 2: We Can Know God by Analyzing Jesus's Character and Ministry 23
Section 3: We Can Know God by Studying Scriptural Prophecy and Revelation 39
Section 4: We Can Know God by Experiencing Human Love and Companionship 55
Section 5: . We Can Know God by Developing Our Own Personal Intuition and Insight 63
Conclusion 77

Introduction

When Paul walked into the city of Athens, he was surprised to find a monument with this inscription: "To an unknown God" (Acts 17:23). He immediately turned to the crowd and began to give them information about the God they were worshiping in ignorance.

Unfortunately, Americans today need spiritual information almost as much as the Greeks needed it then. Honest people will admit that, for the most part, we still worship "an unknown God."

Once, a man asked a young artist, "Sonny, what are you drawing?"

"A picture of God," he replied.

"But no one knows what God looks like," the observer protested.

"Yeah, but they will when I get through," the child declared.

Learning about God is important because everyone needs to know God. Hosea said, "There is…no knowledge of God in the land…. My people are destroyed for lack of knowledge!" (Hos 4:1, 6).

In today's world, information overwhelms us. Communication is constant. People hear about technology, pop culture, sports, and global events immediately. But access to information doesn't translate to knowledge, and the lack of knowledge is especially notable in areas of religion and spirituality. There are several reasons for this: First, new discoveries and fresh insights are discouraged and often forbidden. Sometimes new converts or new ministers are even required to take a sacred vow that they will continue to believe the same dogma, practice the same traditions, and propagate the same teachings for the rest of their lives! Jesus faced this same situation. The Pharisees and Sadducees were stuck in an unproductive system of laws and doctrines and erroneous notions about God. Jesus spent most of his time and energy—and eventually gave his life—trying to correct this false theology. Over and over again, the weight of religion has stood squarely against progressive movements and beneficial innovations such as anesthesia, birth control, and genetic research. Surely such senseless prohibitions result from the worship of an "unknown God."

Then, human brains operate in different ways. Because these organs originated in a primitive era when physical survival was the crucial issue, they handle concrete objects much better than abstract concepts. The lowest level of mental reaction is instinct. Amoebas and other forms of life at this stage of development can only react to stimuli.

The next level is response. Animals and immature human beings tend to act in predetermined ways to meet certain given situations. Robots and computers also operate at this stage of development. The highest level is reason. As mature men and women, we are no longer trapped in a closed system. We are no longer doomed to react by instinct as our DNA code dictates. We're no longer limited to a prescribed set of acceptable responses. Instead, we are free to analyze, discriminate, and choose. This ability to discriminate is what distinguishes human beings from other species. Most animals have a built-in self-preservation mechanism. For instance, if a mother bird senses the touch of human hands, her instinct immediately says, "Danger! Abandon nest!" Normally, this is good advice, but if a baby bird falls to the ground and is returned to the nest by a kind person, then the same life-preserving instinct, which is a protection most of the time, now becomes destructive. It causes the mother bird to avoid that spot, and she may allow her baby to die. In this case instinct becomes the enemy. This even happens to men and women when their bodies reject donated organs.

As human beings we are also limited because we don't have an overall perspective. Most of us view life like one little boy viewed a parade. Since he was too short to see over the fence and too young to leave the yard, he had to look through a knothole. As a result, he saw a lion's head and was afraid. He saw a clown's face and was amused. When he heard a band, he couldn't identify the musicians. When there was a space between floats, he thought the event was over. Evaluating anything on the basis of what little you can personally observe at the present time can be misleading. If the little boy's father had carried him up on the roof, his view would be very different. He would see the beginning of the parade up ahead, the middle of the parade right in front of him, and the end of the parade back down the street. He would have an entirely new perspective. Now he doesn't have to fear the lion, because he can see that it's in a strong cage. He can enjoy the clowns even more because their funny feet are also visible. He can pick out various band instruments, such as the drums, the flutes, and the trombones. A temporary space doesn't fool him into thinking the show is over, because he can plainly see that there are jugglers and acrobats yet to come.

Of course, most of us don't live on a roof with a clear view of life. Instead, our concept of history, our evaluation of circumstances, and our expectations for the future are based solely on what we can see through our own private knothole. This limited outlook can warp our judgment and allow despair to overwhelm us.

God, however, has the rooftop view. The scripture says, "I am God, and there is no one like me, declaring the outcome from the beginning" (Isa 46:9–10). He can enlighten us. James said, "If any of you is lacking in wisdom, ask God, who gives to all generously and ungrudgingly, and it will be given you" (see Jas 1:5).

Christians need to understand complex issues. They need to believe that progress is possible. People will work harder and be more persistent if they know success is attainable. Conversely, their efforts will be minimal if they believe there are some questions without answers, some problems without solutions, or some doors that must not be opened. Knowing God is important, because if you imagine a cruel god, you will also be sadistic. If you imagine a ruthless god, you will also be critical. If you imagine an indecisive, whimsical god, you will also lack integrity. Knowing God is important because you can't have a relationship with someone you don't know.

A wise man said, "Every person has a God-shaped hole in their being, and they can never be happy and successful until it is filled." Most people try desperately to fill that hole with other things. They try to satisfy that emptiness by other means. That can be dangerous. Drugs, alcohol abuse, and pornography are harmful. Pleasure, wealth, and possessions are temporary. Even certain ideas and belief systems can be superstitious and unproductive. In fact, as someone said, "It's often better to know nothing than to know what ain't so."

It's regrettable that gaining knowledge and analyzing information can be a real problem for those dedicated Christians who have been led to believe that questions and doubts are sinful. It's significant that the greatest characters in the Bible were the greatest questioners. This was true of the psalmists, of Job, and of Jeremiah. Even Jesus began and ended his life with questions. At the age of twelve he was seeking information from the theologians in the temple (see Luke 2:46). Then, just before his death on the cross, he was crying out, "Why?" (see Matt 27:46). Questions are legitimate. You can't learn without them. A Chinese proverb states it well: "He who asks a question may seem to be a fool for a moment. But he who doesn't ask a question will remain a fool forever."

The level of maturity we reach and the depth of perception we achieve are not determined by God's willingness to bestow those gifts. Instead, they are determined by our own willingness to receive and utilize them. Suppose two people approach Niagara Falls. One person brings a thimble, and another brings a tub. Who will get the most water? Now, it's not the river's fault that they don't get the same amount. Rather, it's the size of each person's container that determines how much he can receive.

In order to be successful and productive, we need both information and instruction. One philosopher described life as an obscure celestial contest. He said, "It's as if great invisible masters are playing a complicated game. As human spectators, we aren't told the rules or taught the moves. Instead, we're just allowed to watch and then eventually forced to play on a trial-and-error basis."

If we are careful observers, we may begin to link up causes and consequences. We may begin to see consistent patterns. We may begin to comprehend some of the guiding principles. Learning and maturing is a slow and painful process, but that's what growth and discipleship are all about. Many people avoid this arduous undertaking because they are afraid of failure, but the only sure way to never lose is to never play. The only sure way to never fail is to never try. The only sure way to never fall is to never climb. If we continue to avoid all risk and change, then we will remain forever the same, and that will be fatal.

God can help us grow and mature, but in order to utilize divine power, we must align ourselves with universal purposes. Airplanes that align themselves with the winds of the jet stream can benefit greatly.

Their speed increases, and their energy output diminishes. It's important to note, however, that they must adapt to the jet stream; the jet stream doesn't adapt to them. If planes are out of alignment, they won't receive the added boost. And if planes insist upon going in the opposite direction, they will actually be hindered.

Life is the same. If we align ourselves with God's purposes, we benefit, but if we insist upon going in the opposite direction, we'll be hindered. Many things prevent our progress. Lacking confidence and being afraid are big problems. Some fears are legitimate and life-preserving, but others are false and unproductive. If a narrow plank is laying on the ground, we'd probably have no trouble walking along it. But if that same plank was raised one hundred feet into the air, we'd have great difficulty walking along it. What's the difference? The only variable is fear. The height, the possibility of mishap, and the dangers involved affect our physical and mental abilities. Apprehension leads to panic, and panic leads to paralysis.

Then, life's small aggravations can be great obstacles. It's usually the trivial things that try our souls. Some great heroes in war are failures in peace. Some who can stand up to flame and flood are destroyed by tedium. It's the constant daily irritations, not the once-in-a-lifetime catastrophes, that defeat us. Few people experience the dramatic cycles of death, divorce, bankruptcy, and accidents that are portrayed on television, but our little frustrations and disappointments can be just as devastating.

A giant tree that had withstood raging fires and shocking quakes was finally destroyed by tiny, almost microscopic beetles. A little dirt in a gas line stops the car just as surely as a blown engine. One broken cog in a gear can stymy a whole factory. An in-grown toenail or an aching tooth can conquer the bravest of men. Someone has said, "Oh Lord, deliver us from the gnats. We can handle the camels."

Strangely enough, it's probably apathy, inertia, and procrastination that are our greatest hindrances. A certain legend describes an assembly of evil spirits. The dark ruler summons his subjects and asks, "Who will go to earth and persuade men and women to waste their talents and destroy their souls?"

One demon says, "I will go."

"And how will you persuade them?" asks the grim monarch.

"I will persuade them that there is no good in the world."

"That won't do. You'll never be able to force such a belief on mankind."

A second demon speaks up and says, "I will go."

"And how will you persuade them?"

"I will persuade them that there is no evil in the world."

Again, the ruler replies, "That won't do. You'll never convince people of that either. We must have something else, something that will appeal to all ages, classes, and dispositions."

A third evil spirit glides forward and says, "I will go."

"And what will you tell them?"

"I will tell them that indeed there is good and there is evil. I will tell them that indeed choices do make a difference, but I'll also tell them that there is no need to make a choice now. They can always wait until tomorrow."

He was the spirit chosen to go, and that spirit is still with us today. Inaction is one of our greatest temptations. Few of us deliberately choose evil. Few of us get up one morning and decide we are going to harm our family, attack our neighbor, or destroy our country. Instead, we're simply lazy. We live below our possibilities. We fail to understand that the person responsible is us and the time to act is now.

It's true that life can be bewildering and frustrating. Any reasonable person will admit that there are conflicts, mysteries, and irrational events. Good isn't always rewarded, and bad isn't always punished. Work isn't always profitable. Efforts aren't always successful, and returns aren't always commensurate with investments. Chance and sheer luck do seem to play a large role in everyday affairs. Even the writers of scripture sensed this problem. Solomon said, "I saw that under the sun the race is not to the swift, nor the battle to the strong, nor bread to the wise, nor riches to the intelligent, nor favor to the skillful; but time and chance happen to them all" (Eccl 9:11).

Everyone has problems, but these problems can be our teachers. After a terrific downpour, an old farmer was surveying the ruins of his barn. A friend asked what happened. "The roof fell in," said the farmer. "It leaked so long, it just rotted through."

"Why in the world didn't you fix it before it got so bad?"

The old fellow scratched his head, "Well, I just never got around to it. You see, when it was raining, I couldn't work on it. And when the sun was shining, there weren't no need to work on it."

Too many of us are like that farmer. Left to our own devices, we don't constantly press forward. When things are pretty good, we don't automatically seek to make them better. In fact, evil can sometimes be productive by making us so miserable that we will exert the effort to improve. During depression years, people actually become more inventive. Researchers tell us that patent applications invariably go up when economic opportunities go down. Trouble often triggers our ingenuity. The desire to survive and fill unsatisfied needs gives us the will to try.

A little story about a frog makes this point. He fell in a pothole and tried to jump out. After a long while, he thought he couldn't and just gave up. Later, his friends saw him hopping around and said, "We thought you couldn't get out."

"Well, I couldn't," he said, "until I saw this big truck coming and I had to."

We can solve almost anything if we have to.

Religion should encourage human progress. It should not teach its followers that God wants them to be submissive slaves instead of autonomous agents. Analyzing God's character can enable us to understand, respect, and honor him. It's unproductive and dangerous for Christians to continue worshiping an unknown God.

Even so, increasing our knowledge requires effort, because God is probably the most difficult of all words to define. St. Augustine said, "We can know what God is not, but we cannot know what God is." Jesus said, "God is spirit, and God is truth." John said, "God is love." All these descriptive words are concepts or ideas, and people are uncomfortable with ideas—especially profound or complex ideas. In fact, psychologists say that only a small percentage of the population can fully comprehend abstract ideas. Most individuals depend on their senses. They need to see, hear, and touch things in order to know they are real. That's why, for the vast majority of people, sacraments and rituals may be essential spiritual aids. However, we must understand that these aids are not God! All material things are idols. Objects and ceremonies are like fingers pointing to the moon. They may indicate direction, but they must not replace the divine spirit to be worshiped.

People who need personifications of God or symbols for worship usually condemn the few mature believers who don't need them. But those who don't need personifications or symbols often fall into the same trap by ridiculing those people who do need them. We must remember that people who need crutches or braces or insulin should not insist that everyone else must use these things too. But people who don't need these aids most certainly should not deny them to the people who do. It seems we are more sensible and tolerant in physical areas than we are in spiritual areas.

It may surprise some Christians to learn that the most important religious question is not "Do you believe in God?" Rather, the most important question is "What kind of God do you believe in?" That is also a much more difficult question. Many theologians wonder if it's even possible to really know God. But the scripture says that it is possible to know God and to have a relationship with him. Jeremiah says, "When you search for me, you will find me; if you seek me with all your heart" (Jer 29:13).

The words *search* and *seek* mean to ask, to question, and to diligently inquire. They also indicate that the individuals who do this must greatly desire and strive for this knowledge. In the Bible, the word *heart* always deals with expressing deep, honest feelings and using the mental faculties of reason, logic, and analysis. Therefore, let's consider at least five paths we can follow to acquire spiritual understanding:

1. We can know God by observing nature's design and beauty. Scripture says, "The heavens are telling the glory of God; and the firmament proclaims his handiwork. Day to day pours forth speech, and night to night declares knowledge" (Ps 19:1–2).

2. We can know God by analyzing Jesus's character and ministry. Jesus said, "If you know me, you will know my Father also.... Whoever has seen me has seen the Father" (John 14:7, 9).

3. We can know God by studying scriptural prophecy and revelation. The scripture says, "The LORD gives wisdom; from his mouth come knowledge and understanding" (Prov 2:6).

4. We can know God by experiencing human love and companionship. Jesus said, "Everyone will know that you are my disciples, if you have love for one another" (John 13:35).

5. We can know God by developing our own personal intuition and insight. Jesus said, "When the Spirit of truth comes, he will guide you into all the truth" (John 16:13).

Section I

We Can Know God by Observing Nature's Design and Beauty

According to early writers, God spent more time creating the physical elements of the planet than human beings. Light, water, and land were carefully planned and arranged as order replaced chaos. Some critics who complain about "worldly pleasures" don't seem to realize that God doesn't disdain his world. Instead, he believed secular things were important and desirable. The scripture says, "God saw that it was good" (Gen 1:10).

He appreciated the productive activity of trees and vegetation and plants, saying, "Let the earth put forth vegetation: plants yielding seed and fruit trees of every kind on earth that bear fruit with the seed in it" (Gen 1:11). Then he repeated his evaluation, saying it was good (see Gen 1:12).

After observing the sun, the moon, and the stars, God once again examined his work and approved, saying it was good (see Gen 1:18).

In describing the development of higher forms of life, the writer says, "[God said,] 'Let the waters bring forth swarms of living creatures, and let birds fly above the earth across the dome of the sky.' So God created the great sea monsters and every living creature that moves, of every kind, with which the waters swarm and every winged bird of every kind. And God saw that it was good" (Gen 1:20–21).

Finally, God dealt with mammals, including both domestic animals and wild beasts, saying, "'Let the earth bring forth living creatures of every kind: cattle and creeping things and wild animals of the earth of every kind.' And it was so. God made the wild animals of the earth of every kind and the cattle of every kind and everything that creeps upon the ground of every kind. And God saw that it was good" (Gen 1:24–25).

Over and over, the writer emphasizes that God seemed to be pleased with all of these things and pronounced them good.

At the culmination of his work, God delineated the role of men and women, saying, "'Let us make humans in our image, according to our likeness, and let them have dominion over the fish of the sea and over the birds of the air and over the cattle and over all the wild animals of the earth and over every creeping thing that creeps upon the earth.' So God created humans in his image, in the image of God he created them; male and female he created them" (Gen 1:26–27).

Then he gave human beings a specific commandment concerning his creation. The scripture says, "God blessed them, and God said to them, 'Be fruitful and multiply and fill the earth and subdue it and have dominion over the fish of the sea and over the birds of the air and over every living thing that moves upon the earth.'… God saw everything that he had made, and indeed, it was very good" (Gen 1:28, 31).

It's strange that most Christians and many religions disregard these matters. Why do preachers and teachers spend so much of their time warning against other sins, such as pornography or heresy, and seldom mention the fact that men and women have been given the specific command to manage and protect our world? We've neglected and abused most of the gifts God has given us. Global warming is one serious problem, but endangered species, loss of our forests, pollution in our rivers, and wasteful habits are other problems. Even littering and failing to recycle are insults to our creator.

The well-known story of Noah's Ark also emphasizes God's concern for his animals. The scripture says, "Of every living thing, of all flesh, you shall bring two of every kind into the ark, to keep them alive with you; they shall be male and female. Of the birds according to their kinds and of the animals after their kinds, of every creeping thing of the ground according to its kind, two of every kind shall come in to you, to keep them alive. Also take with you every kind of food that is eaten, and store it up; and it shall serve as food for you and for them" (Gen 6:19–21).

These ancient scripture passages teach us about God's creation and how he cares for it. They even give a description of one of his most colorful and interesting symbols. As a reminder of the covenant, God gave them a rainbow and said, "I have set my bow in the clouds, and it shall be a sign of the covenant between me and the earth. When I bring clouds over the earth and the bow is seen in the clouds, I will remember my covenant that is between me and you and every living creature of all flesh, and the waters shall never again become a flood to destroy all flesh. When the bow is in the clouds, I will see it and remember the everlasting covenant between God and every living creature" (Gen 9:13–16).

The scriptures indicate that things of the earth can teach us about God: "Ask the animals, and they will teach you, the birds of the air, and they will tell you; ask the plants of the earth, and they will teach you, and the fish of the sea will declare to you" (Job 12:7–8).

Many other scriptures give details about God's relationship with his earthly creatures. One verse promises, "All the earth shall be filled with the glory of the LORD" (Num 14:21).

The psalmists present several praise passages: "The earth is the LORD's and all that is in it, the world, and those who live in it" (Ps 24:1); "O LORD, how manifold are your works! In wisdom you have made them all; the earth is full of your creatures. There is the sea, great and wide; creeping things innumerable are there, living things both small and great" (Ps 104:24–25); "Praise him, sun and moon; praise him all you shining stars! Praise him, you highest heavens and the waters above the heavens" (Ps 148:3–4).

Jeremiah assures us of God's permanent presence: "Do I not fill the heaven and earth? says the LORD" (Jer 23:24).

Solomon compliments the pleasing features of nature, saying, "He has made everything suitable for its time" (Eccl 3:11); "The flowers appear on the earth; the time of singing has come, and the voice of the turtledove is heard in our land" (Song of Songs 2:12).

Isaiah says, "The desert shall rejoice and blossom" (Isa 35:1). Isaiah also quotes God in a song of praise, saying, "Sing, O heavens, for the LORD has done it; shout, O depths of the earth; break forth into singing, O mountains, O forest and every tree in it!" (Isa 44:23). Later, he says, "You shall go out in joy and be led back in peace; the mountains and the hills before you shall burst into song, and all the trees of the field shall clap their hands" (Isa 55:12).

These poetic and artistic verses show us that God is not merely a strict moralist establishing a list of rules or a stern judge meting out punishment. Rather, they describe God as a passionate and protective caretaker.

Solomon even used insects to teach us about planning. He said, "Go to the ant, you lazybones; consider its ways, and be wise. Without having any chief or officer or ruler, it prepares its food in summer, and gathers its sustenance in harvest" (Prov 6:6–8). These ants certainly have better work habits than many people do.

God gave Job special information about creation and shared knowledge about the operation of the universe. He began by asking, "Where were you when I laid the foundation of the earth?" Then the author of Job offers almost two chapters of detailed explanations concerning God's interaction with nature. He asks, "Have you ever in your life commanded the morning and caused the dawn to know its place? Have you entered into the springs of the sea? Or have you walked in the recesses of the deep? Where is the way to the dwelling of light? And darkness, where is its place? Have you entered the storehouses of the snow, or have you seen the storehouses of the hail, where is the way that the light is divided, or the east wind scattered on the earth? Who has cleft the channel for the flood, or a way for the thunderbolt to bring rain on the land or make the seeds of grass to sprout, who has begotten the drops of dew?" He also explained something about seasons and temperature changes, saying, "Water becomes hard like stone" (see Job 38–39).

God discussed astronomy by asking, "Can you bind the chains of the Pleiades or loose the cords of Orion? Can you lead forth the Mazzaroth in their season, or can you guide the Bear with its children?... Can you send forth lightnings?" (Job 38:31–32, 35).

At this point God began to deal with wildlife, asking,

> Can you hunt the prey for the lion or satisfy the appetite of the young lions, when they crouch in their dens or lie in wait in their covert? Who provides for the raven its prey, when its young ones cry to God and wander about for lack of food? Do you know when the mountain goats give birth? Do you observe the calving of the deer? Can you number the months that they fulfill, and do you

know the time when they give birth, when they crouch to give birth to their offspring and are delivered of their young? Their young ones become strong; they grow up in the open; they go forth and do not return to them. Who has let the wild ass go free? Who has loosed the bonds of the swift ass, to which I have given the steppe for its home, the salt land for its dwelling place?... Is the wild ox willing to serve you? Will it spend the night at your crib? Can you tie it in the furrow with ropes, or will it harrow the valleys after you? (Job 38:39–39:6, 9–10)

He continues to give interesting observations about birds, saying,

> The ostrich's wings flap wildly, though its pinions lack plumage. For it leaves its eggs to the earth and lets them be warmed on the ground, forgetting that a foot may crush them and that a wild animal may trample them. It deals cruelly with its young, as if they were not its own; though its labor should be in vain, yet it has no fear; because God has made it forget wisdom.... Is it by your wisdom that the hawk soars and spreads its wings toward the south? Is it at your command that the eagle mounts up and makes its nest on high? It lives on the rock and makes its home in the fastness of the rocky crag. From there it spies the prey; its eyes see it from far away." (Job 39:13–17, 26–29)

This lengthy and astonishing conversation with Job doesn't give us much useful information about biology or physics. It certainly doesn't impart any great insights about theology. But it does show us that God has a great interest in nature and science. It reminds us that God is an involved creator and wants us to be knowledgeable and protective of creation.

Later, Jesus uses a mother hen and her babies to illustrate God's love and care for his people: "Jerusalem, Jerusalem, the city that kills the prophets and stones those who are sent to it! How often have I desired to gather your children as a hen gathers her brood under her wings, and you were not willing!" (Matt 23:37).

Jesus also describes God's concern for animals, saying, "If one of you has a child or an ox that has fallen into a well, will you not immediately pull him out on a Sabbath day?" (Luke 14:5).

He reminds us that we must care for our animals, saying, "Does not each of you on the Sabbath untie his ox or his donkey from the manger and lead it to water?" (Luke 13:15).

Then, specifically, Jesus refers to an insignificant creature, saying, "Are not five sparrows sold for two pennies? Yet not one of them is forgotten in God's sight" (Luke 12:6).

Jesus often uses the analogy of a shepherd and sheep to explain God's love and concern for us: "Suppose one of you has only one sheep and it falls into a pit on the Sabbath; will you not lay hold of it and lift it out?" (Matt 12:11); "Which one of you, having a hundred sheep and losing one of them, does not leave the ninety-nine in the wilderness and go after the one that is lost until he finds it?" (Luke 15:4).

Jesus describes a God who appreciates beauty when he asks his followers, "Why do you worry about clothing? Consider the lilies of the field, how they grow; they neither toil nor spin, yet I tell you, even Solomon in all his glory was not clothed like one of these. But if God so clothes the grass of the field, which is alive today and tomorrow is thrown into the oven, will he not much more clothe you—you of little faith?" (Matt 6:28–30).

There are hints about God's creative ability and special concern for the natural elements throughout the scriptures. Even so, these details are seldom mentioned in descriptions about God. We really do not know God.

The reason God remains unknown—the reason spirituality includes so much superstition and the reason religion is so misunderstood—is probably because abstract concepts are difficult to express. Using concrete material in analogies can clear up some of these false beliefs. That's why Jesus used so many parables.

God's character may also be misrepresented because our language is imprecise. Certain passages seem to indicate that God can be regretful, wrathful, or vindictive. We must discount such misleading statements and reinterpret their real meaning. We already do this in the physical realm. For instance, when meteorologists say, "The sun isn't shining today," we know that's not true. The sun doesn't choose which times and which days it is going to shine. That's nonsense! The sun simply shines. That's all it can do. It shines through our days and our nights and our eclipses and our storms. So when we say, "The sun isn't shining today," that's not a literal statement. We mean we're not seeing or experiencing the sun at this moment. Of course the sun is shining, but the rotation of the earth, the alignment of the moon, the presence of the clouds, or our own position here on earth determines whether we are personally seeing and experiencing that sunshine.

It's the same with language about God. God doesn't have emotional meltdowns. God doesn't have bad moods or make mistakes. God specifically declares, "I the LORD do not change" (Mal 3:6).

God is love. That's all he is! It's life's circumstances and our own choices that cause different consequences and outcomes.

Christians who worship an unknown God must become more knowledgeable about that God. Christians who live in a technological world must become more knowledgeable about that world.

The old adage "What you don't know can't hurt you" is false and often leads to tragedy. A rancher once said, "I don't have much trouble with a break in the fence that I know about. I can keep my cows away from that area until it can be repaired. It's those gaps I don't know about that cause all the trouble." Likewise, it's those laws of God and nature we don't know about that cause all the trouble. Years ago, scientists didn't know that the overuse of insecticides would imbalance nature. If we had understood these principles, we could have prevented many problems.

Ancient thinkers and writers were uninformed. They had few scientific and technological resources, so their erroneous responses are understandable. We're much better informed today. Therefore, superstitious and erroneous claims on our part are not understandable. In fact, they are inexcusable. Any deliberate ignorance of God and God's world is sinful.

Nevertheless, learning is not easy. It has taken years, centuries, and indeed eons to put together even a few pieces of the cosmic puzzle, and the picture is still far from complete. But we do have more knowledge than our ancestors. Without factual information or technical equipment, it was inevitable that they would make invalid assumptions. For example, thunder, lightning, hail, tornadoes, earthquakes, and volcano eruptions were once attributed to the moods and actions of powerful gods. Jesus repudiated some of those beliefs about the weather when he said, "Love your enemies and pray for those who persecute you, so that you may be children of your Father in heaven, for he makes his sun rise on the evil and on the good and sends rain on the righteous and the unrighteous" (Matt 5:44–45). This statement assures us that nature is neutral. The sun and rain and storms are not controlled by divine whims. A psalmist verifies this by explaining that the seasons are determined by natural principles: "You established the luminaries and the sun. You have fixed all the bounds of the earth; you made summer and winter" (Ps 74:16–17).

Many of the prophets had also begun to express a better understanding of God. Elijah discovered one of the most important spiritual principles when he realized that nature and God are not synonymous. The scripture says, "'The LORD is about to pass by!'… There was a great wind, so strong that it was splitting mountains and breaking rocks in pieces before the LORD, but the LORD was not in the wind, and after the wind an earthquake, but the LORD was not in the earthquake, and after the earthquake a fire, but the LORD was not in the fire, and after the fire a sound of sheer silence" (1 Kgs 19:11–13).

In these early days misconceptions were common. Almost every unusual event was labeled a miracle. Even centuries later, when primitive tribesmen saw their first hot air balloon, they immediately attributed its rise to a supernatural force. Since they knew very little about scientific laws, this conclusion seemed logical.

That same response is sometimes still used today. When things happen that don't have an obvious and recognizable cause, many people claim they are supernatural miracles. Television, cellphones, and the internet would probably all be labeled as miracles if we had not observed their development and if we didn't understand, to some degree, how they operate.

Other false beliefs cause even more misery. Personal problems and human tragedies were once thought to be punishments from an angry God. For instance, when a couple was childless, people assumed God was denying them the blessing of parenthood. We now know that blocked fallopian tubes, low sperm count, infections, and other biological factors all contribute to infertility. Since many of these conditions can be remedied by surgery or medication, it's obvious that God's will is not the cause of barrenness. When Jesus said to the young man at the temple, "You are not blind because of your sin or your parent's sin," he released that afflicted man from a tremendous burden of guilt (see John 9:1–3). When he said to the poor stooped woman, "You're not afflicted by God, but by Satan," he opened up an entirely new realm of hope (see Luke 13:11–16). These welcomed reassurances were repeated over and over again. Jesus, in essence, kept saying, "You do not deserve illness and limitation. You are entitled to wholeness and happiness. That's your birthright! That's God's desire for you!"

Religion exacerbates another problem when it tries to separate God from the world. Someone with an inquiring mind asked several fascinating questions: Is God as interested in rabbits as he is in angels? Is God as concerned about research labs as he is about churches? Is God as disturbed about pollution as he is about promiscuity?

These questions may astonish traditional Christians. It never occurs to most of us that God is interested in animal husbandry even though God created living things and gave us dominion over them. It never occurs to us that God is concerned with genetic research even though God created human beings and gave them a commission to be productive. It never occurs to us that God is disturbed about soil erosion even though God created the earth and vegetation and told us to use them well. We've so separated God from the universe that we don't even think of God as an awesome creator. We just think of God as a moralistic rule keeper.

Let's remember that, in the beginning, God spent the vast majority of his time and effort on this natural world, and the scriptures say God was pleased with this work! If this is true, why wouldn't God be just as interested and concerned and disturbed about our actions in the areas of geology, astronomy, and biology as our behavior in the area of religion? The song says, "This is my Father's world." Either all of it is of God or none of it is of God!

God inspires scientists working with microscopes just as surely as he inspires preachers working with sermons. God calls physicists to analyze nuclear elements just as surely as he calls theologians to analyze Greek and Hebrew texts. God guides the anthropologist just as surely as he guides the missionary.

So God is interested in rabbits, research labs, and pollution. In a unified universe, compartmentalization stymies us. When we separate areas of life into categories, progress is impossible. When we divide matters of the world from matters of the spirit, we can't make the connections that are necessary to solve many of life's problems. That's why discovering and understanding both physical and spiritual laws is crucial in today's world. There are no taboo areas, unknowable mysteries, or restricted zones that are forbidden to mortals. Scientists and inventors don't have to be afraid that they are playing God when they try new things. On the contrary, our main task is to increase our knowledge in all areas. We must find the causes of our difficulties and the solutions to our problems. Believing that it is both possible and permissible to discover God's laws is important. Jesus said, "To you it has been given to know the secrets of the kingdom of God" (Luke 8:10).

God's character, principles, and purposes are complex, and his methods of operation are complicated. But a few facts are evident: God is reasonable. Creation is orderly. The world and nature are evidence of God's tremendous ability. Einstein expressed this belief when he said, "God does not play dice with the universe." Scripture says, "The heavens are telling the glory of God, and the firmament proclaims his handiwork" (Ps 19:1). That's so true! No person can wander out in a rural area on a clear night and not be impressed by the starry sky. We marvel at the majestic mountains and are mesmerized by the crashing waves of the ocean. We're amazed by the changing seasons, the winter snow, the spring flowers, the summer gardens, and the autumn leaves. What a wonderful world!

Scientists can depend on the consistent natural laws that control everything from the orbits of the planets to the atoms in our brains. Those brains are so efficient and brilliant that they have enabled us to develop television, which sends pictures through the air; cellphones, which allow us to hear voices of people who are thousands of miles away; the internet, with its overwhelming quantity of information. These brains have even given ordinary men and women the ability to explore space and to walk on the moon.

Nature teaches us about the intricate, fascinating scientific principles and technical possibilities of our world. It reveals a hopeful outlook that evaluates all the elements of the universe as being good. It also emphasizes the beauty and harmony of our surroundings. Such a creator must be intelligent and technically astute. When he evaluated his work, he was pleased. He must also be aesthetic and artistic since he valued the colors and symmetry of his rainbow. Later, Jesus expressed admiration for lovely flowers, saying, "Consider the lilies of the field…even Solomon in all his glory was not clothed like one of these" (Matt 6:28, 29). God can't be a petty autocrat who sits on a throne trying to decide which mindless rituals he wants his subjects to perform or which painful penalties he will impose on those helpless creatures who happen to break a rule or make a mistake.

It's fortunate that we can begin to know and appreciate God by observing nature's design and beauty.

Section 2

We Can Know God by Analyzing Jesus's Character and Ministry

If knowing Jesus is the same as knowing God, then God's character must be like Jesus's character. God's principles must be like Jesus's principles. God's purposes must be like Jesus's purposes. This is important knowledge because it assures us that the way Jesus treated others is the way God treats us. Therefore, let's consider several significant incidents that will help us understand Jesus's personality traits and methods of dealing with people.

Once, Jesus met a wealthy man with a high government position. He had a nice home, good food, and all the luxuries of life. But several factors combined to make him feel inadequate. In that day, respectable Jewish society ostracized those fellow Jews who collected taxes for Rome. Not only did these "traitors" collaborate with the hated foreigners, but most were also guilty of using their position to extort extra money for themselves. As a chief tax collector, Zacchaeus was able to practice this extortion in an entire district. Also, this publican was short. People probably ridiculed his size, and this, plus his unethical lifestyle, made him feel defensive and miserable.

Then, one day, Zacchaeus was confronted with his moment of decision. He heard that a certain teacher was traveling through his village. He was interested and wanted to see this man for himself, but he faced a dilemma: The crowd was large, and the taller spectators blocked his view. As a person used to solving problems, he ran ahead and climbed up a tree. It wasn't the most dignified behavior, but Zacchaeus was desperate.

Zacchaeus's desire to see Jesus was more than mere curiosity. He was a serious seeker. Now, Zacchaeus probably wouldn't have used the word *lost* to describe himself; but he was definitely aware that something was wrong. He also knew his wealth couldn't make it right.

When Jesus saw the expectant look on Zacchaeus's face, he greeted him by name and offered to become a guest in his home. Zacchaeus quickly responded. Of course, many religious people criticized Jesus for associating with such a notorious sinner, but neither Jesus nor Zacchaeus was deterred by his critics. Zacchaeus's radical change is demonstrated in both words and deeds. He gave half of his goods to the poor, and he pledged fourfold restitution to anyone he had defrauded. Jesus said, "Today salvation has come to this house" (Luke 19:9).

The theology of that era tended to describe salvation primarily in future terms. People hoped to be declared righteous at the final judgment. But Jesus referred to salvation as a present reality. Zacchaeus gladly accepted the grace God offered in spite of the hostility of his self-righteous critics. He was willing to rearrange his priorities and use his possessions productively. He realized he was being given an opportunity to start over, and his life was changed.

Now, what does this account of Jesus's interaction with Zacchaeus reveal about God? Well, it shows us that God has a great concern for sinners and proves that God will immediately accept and forgive us if we're serious seekers. It also demonstrates that God's grace can enable us to alter our attitudes and behavior.

Jesus met another person who had terrible personal problems. One after another of this woman's five marriages had collapsed. Abuse and infidelity had worn her down, and now she didn't even bother with legal arrangements. Instead, she simply lived with men. Because of her numerous relationships and illicit sexual episodes, she was the victim of gossip. The proper women shunned and scorned her.

Coming to the village well every day was an unpleasant experience for this woman. Normally, women gathered at this social center in the cool of the morning or evening. This woman probably came at noon so she wouldn't have to face her neighbors. But one day when she arrived, expecting to draw water, the woman at the well was confronted with her moment of decision. The conversation that ensued had even greater barriers than usual. In the first place, it was a man who spoke to her, and this was strange. Furthermore, he was a Jew, and she was a Samaritan.

These groups had experienced decades of racial animosity. Orthodox Jews usually avoided this whole area, but Jesus had chosen to rest here while his disciples went into the village to buy food.

When Jesus asked the woman for a drink, she was surprised. In her culture men didn't speak to women in public, and certainly not to women of questionable morals. Then Jesus indicated that if she only knew him, she would ask for living water. That phrase referred to a fresh, flowing stream, rather than the more stagnant water from a well. It's obvious Jesus had a deeper meaning in mind. The living water he offered was symbolic of spiritual truth that led to eternal life.

The woman took Jesus's offer literally and asked how he could draw water when he didn't have a rope. Jesus told her a drink from this well would only quench physical thirst for a short time; those who drank living water would never have to drink again. Perhaps, remembering her embarrassing daily visits to the well, she immediately expressed a desire for this wonderful water. But when Jesus asked her to call her husband, she was forced to admit she had lived with several men and wasn't even married to her present partner. Surprisingly, Jesus didn't condemn her, but the discussion had become uncomfortable, so the woman did what a lot of us would do—she changed the subject, bringing up an old theological issue about the proper place to worship God. The Jews insisted worship must be centered in the temple at Jerusalem, and the Samaritans worshiped on a special mountain.

In his answer, Jesus changed the whole idea of worship forever by emphasizing its spiritual and mental aspects. He dismissed any idea of sacred buildings or special rituals or required ceremonies. Instead, he said, "True worshipers will worship the Father in spirit and truth" (John 4:23).

At that point the woman left her water pot behind and became a witness to others. The report of Jesus's conversation with this woman reveals that God desires to reach out to all nationalities and genders. Samaritans were considered heretics, and this one also had many moral faults and social problems, but she wasn't reprimanded or punished. Instead, she was treated with respect and offered new life. God doesn't regard women as second-class citizens or inferior in any way. Jesus didn't hesitate to discuss deep theological matters with her. In fact, he shared one of his most significant doctrines by telling her that God is to be worshiped in spirit and in truth. It doesn't matter if we're male or female; it doesn't matter if we're of a different culture or a different religion. God will still accept and honor us.

It's important to note that even though Jesus did come to help poor, unlearned outcasts, he also interacted with educated people. Once, a man came to see Jesus. He was a scholar, as well as a legal authority, with a lot of prestige and financial security. He was intelligent and well respected. This man, Nicodemus, was a member of the Sanhedrin, the highest Jewish court. Jesus called him "a teacher of Israel," indicating he was a trained theologian. If anyone could please God by having scriptural knowledge and by keeping all the laws, surely it was Nicodemus.

As a Pharisee, Nicodemus was religious, but it's obvious he wanted something more. He may have come at night because of embarrassment or in order to avoid the crowds, but probably that was the only time for these two busy men to have an uninterrupted conversation. We know Nicodemus had observed Jesus's ministry because he called him "Rabbi," which was a title of honor. He also said, "We know that God is with you."

Ignoring these compliments, Jesus got straight to the heart of the matter, saying, "To see the kingdom of God a person has to be born from above." This startling statement shocked Nicodemus. People like him traced their lineage back to Abraham. They kept the law, studied the prophets, and lived in expectation of the coming kingdom. Jesus was telling him that he couldn't even see this kingdom of God, much less enter it, without a new birth. Interpreting this statement literally, Nicodemus asked, "How can a grown person be born again?" Jesus responded with a spiritual analogy. Using the Hebrew word that meant both wind and spirit, he explained that although we can't see the wind, we can tell it's real by experiencing its effects. Likewise, we can know that the new birth is real by experiencing its effect.

Nicodemus's immediate response is not recorded, but Scripture later relates that he spoke out in Jesus's defense and was accused of being a follower. Then, after the crucifixion, Nicodemus asked Pilate for permission to remove Jesus's body from the cross. The scriptures say Nicodemus and his friend "took the body of Jesus and wrapped it with the spices in linen cloths, according to the burial custom of the Jews" (John 19:40). Without this intervention by Nicodemus and Joseph of Arimathea, Jesus's body would have been thrown into a common pit with the bodies of the thieves. Since Nicodemus put his position and his life on the line, we know he must have accepted Jesus's explanation of the gospel.

This significant discussion shows us that God reaches out to rich and famous and academically oriented individuals. He knows that even religious leaders can have spiritual problems, and he wants all of us to be willing to start over if we realize we're on the wrong path. Jesus's ministry was varied. It's obvious he was not partial to certain types of people, because he also dealt with one person who was exactly opposite to Nicodemus in every way. This poor man had fallen about as low as he could go. He was so deranged that he was treated as an animal. Totally cast out from ordinary life, he lived among the dead. The place he inhabited was considered an area of defilement.

The physical, emotional, and social conditions of the demoniac were deplorable. He had been restrained with chains, but he broke them and ran away. The powers that possessed him were so strong that he called himself Legion (this term represented a Roman army unit of six thousand men). He was both feared and despised by his neighbors and had become so self-destructive that he cut himself with stones. His case seemed hopeless, but it wasn't.

When Jesus and his disciples reached Gentile territory in a boat and stepped ashore, they saw this wild creature running toward them. Something was drawing him to Jesus. The crazed part of him saw Jesus as an enemy, but a spark of humanity remained. Like so many psychotic individuals, he was torn between wanting help and rejecting it. Even as he knelt, his body language begged for assistance, but his words contradicted his plea. He was both terrified and enraged: "He cried out and fell down before him, shouting, 'What have you to do with me, Jesus, Son of the Most High God? I beg you, do not torment me'" (Luke 8:28).

This man was afraid to trust Jesus, but fortunately he didn't let fear hold him back. There have been many attempts to explain why Jesus may have indicated that his condition could be transferred to the swine. One explanation is that Jesus did this so the man would have concrete evidence that the evil had departed from him. But the most disturbing aspect of this encounter was the reaction of the local people. Many of them knew this demoniac. They had probably cursed him and avoided him. When they saw him "sitting at the feet of Jesus, clothed and in his right mind," they should have been grateful and happy, but instead they felt threatened and ordered Jesus to leave. Change, even when it's positive, almost always causes anxiety and resentment.

The man himself begged to go with Jesus. He felt great loyalty to his healer and was more secure in his presence. Furthermore, he was probably reluctant to stay there and deal with his hateful neighbors. But Jesus told him to go home and tell others what God had done for him. This incident that describes Jesus's concern for the demoniac gives us dramatic evidence that God desires to help everyone, even those with serious mental disabilities and social problems. Later, we see that Jesus didn't hesitate when approached by criminals. The man being executed on the cross beside him was a detriment to society. Now he had been arrested and sentenced to death. He knew he was guilty and readily admitted his illegal activities and sins. For him, life was over. It certainly seemed too late for another chance. There was no time for a retrial or a pardon. In fact, his execution was already being carried out. You'd think this man would have given up in despair, but suddenly the thief on the cross was confronted with his moment of decision. In speaking of this story, a pastor warned his congregation that the scripture recorded the last-minute conversion of one thief to give us hope, but it recorded only one such conversion so we wouldn't be presumptuous.

This thief's earnest request raises the question of why some people believe and some don't. Two thieves were being executed. Both of them had apparently been exposed to the same sights and sounds. It seems they were equally culpable, yet one joined in the mockery of Jesus, and the other believed and honored the Lord. The penitent thief expressed an amazing faith. At the darkest hour, when he was suffering, he asked for mercy. At a time when things seemed to be hopeless, even to Jesus's closest followers, this man reached out in faith. It's likely he had a limited experience with religion. He probably hadn't had the advantage of observing Jesus's ministry, witnessing his miracles, or hearing him preach. He probably didn't understand much of the gospel message, but somehow he realized Jesus could help him. When the thief asked to be remembered in the coming kingdom, Jesus immediately promised he would be with him in paradise on that very day.

The powerful effect of Jesus's promise to the thief assures us that it's never too late for God to offer grace. It also provides proof that God doesn't require good works or sacred rituals or any other action on our part. Salvation is free.

In Jesus's interaction with these individuals, he was representing God. That's why he said, "You can learn about God by observing me." In order to benefit from this knowledge, we must study each incident in Jesus's life to find the deeper meaning. For instance, in his first public message at Nazareth, he made two controversial points. When he read from the scriptures and repeated accepted doctrines, the people "spoke well of him and were amazed at his gracious words." But when he mentioned two non-Hebrew and non-orthodox individuals, and dared to say God had cared for them and given them a special blessing, the people were furious. The portion of his sermon that caused the violent reaction was when he said,

> There were many widows in Israel in the time of Elijah, when the heaven was shut up three years and six months and there was a severe famine over all the land, yet Elijah was sent to none of them except to a widow at Zarephath in Sidon. There were also many with a skin disease in Israel in the time of the prophet Elisha, and none of them was cleansed except Naaman the Syrian. When they heard this, all in the synagogue were filled with rage. They got up, drove him out of the town, and led him to the brow of the hill on which their town was built, so that they might hurl him off the cliff." (Luke 4:25–29)

In his teachings and stories, Jesus always emphasized the fact that God loves and blesses all types of people. He is not partial to the elite. Even in Jesus's parables of the feasts, there is an absence of racial or national prejudice. He said, "People will come from east and west, from north and south, and take their places at the banquet in the kingdom of God" (Luke 13:29).

When he visited Mary and Martha, Jesus repudiated the common gender bias and supported Mary when she chose to discuss theology instead of working in the kitchen. The scripture says, "[Martha] had a sister named Mary, who sat at the Jesus's feet and listened to what he was saying. But Martha was distracted by her many tasks, so she came to him and asked, 'Lord, do you not care that my sister has left me to do all the work by myself? Tell her, then, to help me.' But the Lord answered her, 'Martha, Martha, you are worried and distracted by many things, but few things are needed—indeed only one. Mary has chosen the better part, which will not be taken away from her'" (Luke 10:39–42).

From Jesus's words and actions in these accounts, we can be sure that he, and therefore God, wants us to know that divine favor can reach all cultures and offer equal opportunities to both men and women. When people live in a diverse world, it's important for them to believe and practice that principle.

Above all else, Jesus was a teacher. He came to impart wisdom. He came to enlighten a dark world. He came to correct false ideas. At his trial Jesus told Pilate he had come into the world to bear witness to the truth (see John 18:37). He especially came to teach us the truth about God. This included helping us to know God and to discover what he wants us to do. Jesus fulfilled his purpose by demonstrating with his life.

Since Jesus was sensible, practical, and productive, we know God expects us to be sensible, practical, and productive. His advice to those who are always looking for miracles and signs is blunt. When a group asked him to show them a sign from heaven, he answered them by saying, "An evil and adulterous generation asks for a sign, but no sign will be given to it" (Matt 16:4).

Jesus also disregarded trivial rules about eating with unwashed hands. He said, "Do you not see that whatever goes into the mouth enters the stomach and goes out into the sewer? But what comes out of the mouth proceeds from the heart, and this is what defiles. For out of the heart come evil intentions, murder, adultery, sexual immorality, theft, false witness, and slander. These are what defile a person, but to eat with unwashed hands does not defile" (Matt 15:17–20).

The Pharisees were fanatical about observing the Sabbath, but Jesus wasn't. Once on a Sabbath day, as they made their way through the grain fields, Jesus's disciples began to pluck heads of grain. The Pharisees said to him, "Look, why are they doing what is not lawful on the Sabbath?" And he said to them, "Have you never read what David did when he and his companions were hungry and in need of food, how he entered the house of God…and ate the bread of the Presence, which it is not lawful for any but the priests to eat, and he gave some to his companions?" Then he said to them, "The Sabbath was made for humankind and not humankind for the Sabbath." (Mark 2:23–27)

In other words, the commandments and religious rules were given for the benefit of human beings. Human beings were not created for the specific purpose of obeying commandments and rules.

Jesus is stereotyped as a religious figure with a halo and white robes. But he neither used nor advocated pious language. Furthermore, he was abrupt with a woman who gave him an effusive compliment. The scripture says that while he was preaching, "A woman in the crowd raised her voice and said to him, 'Blessed is the womb that bore you and the breasts that nursed you!' But he said, 'Blessed rather are those who hear the word of God and obey it!'" (Luke 11:27–28).

If Jesus really reflected God's attitudes, then perhaps we should rethink some of our methods of worship. Millions of well-meaning Christians who believe shouting and singing praise choruses is especially pleasing to God may be mistaken.

One of Jesus's parables proves that God is much more interested in works than words: "A man had two sons; he went to the first and said, 'Son, go and work in the vineyard today.' He answered, 'I will not,' but later he changed his mind and went. The father went to the second and said the same, and he answered, 'I go, sir,' but he did not go. Which of the two did the will of his father?' They said, 'the first'" (Matt 21:28–31). They were right!

Of course, Jesus constantly emphasized love and acceptance, but he also taught about God's tough love. He assured us that God doesn't want us to waste time with unresponsive people and unprofitable situations, saying, "Whenever you enter a town and they do not welcome you, go out into its streets and say, 'Even the dust of your town that clings to our feet, we wipe off in protest against you'" (Luke 10:10–11). He also said, "Do not give what is holy to dogs, and do not throw your pearls before swine, or they will trample them under foot and turn and maul you" (Matt 7:6).

The cleansing of the temple episode is another example of God's tough love in action. The scripture says, "Jesus entered the temple and drove out all those who were selling and buying in the temple, and he overturned the tables of the money changers and the seats of those who sold doves. He said to them, 'It is written, "My house shall be called a house of prayer," but you are making it a den of robbers'" (Matt 21:12–13).

Many of Jesus's parables and lessons show us that God expects us to be productive and efficient. The story of the ten virgins emphasizes planning and preparation. He said,

> Ten young women took their lamps and went to meet the bridegroom. Five of them were foolish, and five were wise. When the foolish took their lamps, they took no oil with them, but the wise took flasks of oil with their lamps. As the bridegroom was delayed, all of them became drowsy and slept. But at midnight there was a shout, "Look! Here is the bridegroom! Come out to meet him." Then all those young women got up and trimmed their lamps. The foolish said to the wise, "Give us some of your oil, for our lamps are going out." But the wise replied, "No! there will not be enough for you and for us; you had better go to the dealers and buy some for yourselves." And while they went to buy it, the bridegroom came, and those who were ready went with him into the wedding banquet, and the door was shut. Later the other young women came also, saying, "Lord, lord, open to us." But he replied, "Truly I tell you, I do not know you." (Matt 25:1–12)

The account of a man begging for bread from his neighbor advises us to be persistent. Jesus said,

> Suppose one of you has a friend, and you go to him at midnight and say to him, "Friend, lend me three loaves of bread, for a friend of mine has arrived, and I have nothing to set before him." And he answers from within, "Do not bother me; the door has already been locked, and my children are with me in bed; I cannot get up and give you anything." I tell you, even though he will not get up and give him anything out of friendship, at least because of his persistence he will get up and give him whatever he needs. (Luke 11:5–8)

This doesn't mean God is reluctant to respond to our requests or that he wants us to beg. That's just how life works; it rewards determination and perseverance.

The example of a barren tree deals with idleness and provides more evidence of God's tough love: "A man had a fig tree planted in his vineyard, and he came looking for fruit on it and found none. So he said to the man working the vineyard, 'See here! For three years I have come looking for fruit on this fig tree, and still I find none. Cut it down! Why should it be wasting the soil?'" (Luke 13:6–7).

The encounter with a man at the pool illustrates the benefit of showing initiative and independence. Jesus told about a pool called Beth-zatha. Many invalids—blind, lame, and paralyzed—lay in its porticoes. One man was there who had been ill for thirty-eight years. Jesus knew he had been there for a long time, so he said to him, "'Do you want to be made well?' The ill man answered him, 'Sir, I have no one to put me into the pool when the water is stirred up, and while I am making my way, someone else steps down ahead of me.' Jesus said to him, 'Stand up, take your mat and walk.' At once the man was made well, and he took up his mat and began to walk" (see John 5:2–9).

The parable of the talents proves that actions and even risk can be better than extreme caution. One man did not invest the money, and his master said to him, "You wicked and lazy slave!... You ought to have invested my money with the bankers, and on my return I would have received my own with interest. So take the talent from him, and give it to the one with the ten talents.... As for this worthless slave, throw him into outer darkness, where there will be weeping and gnashing of teeth" (see Matt 25:26–30).

In the feeding of the five thousand, frugality is seen as a virtue: "All ate and were filled, and they took up what was left over of the broken pieces, twelve baskets full" (Matt 14:20).

Jesus certainly taught that God wants us to be kind and helpful. His famous story about the good Samaritan emphasizes the importance of concern for others. Two religious leaders passed by an injured victim, "But a Samaritan while traveling came upon him, and when he saw him he was moved with compassion. He went to him and bandaged his wounds, treating them with oil and wine. Then he put him on his own animal, brought him to an inn, and took care of him. The next day he took out two denarii, gave them to the innkeeper, and said, 'Take care of him, and when I come back I will repay you whatever more you spend'" (Luke 10:33–35). God cares about our welfare.

Surprisingly, Jesus seemed to approve of assertive individuals more than he did of submissive individuals. Once, a foreign woman dared to give Jesus a rather impudent response and was rewarded. When this Gentile begged him to cast a demon out of her daughter, he said to her, "'Let the children be fed first, for it not fair to take the children's food and throw it to the dogs.' But she answered him, 'Sir, even the dogs under the table eat the children's crumbs.' Then he said to her, 'For saying that, you may go—the demon has left your daughter'" (Mark 7:27–29). Now, if God is like Jesus, then this little episode gives us an interesting insight into God's attitude toward strong-willed individuals. He does not want us to be weak and passive.

At a wedding in Cana, Jesus helped an embarrassed host:

> Jesus and his disciples had also been invited to the wedding. When the wine gave out, the mother of Jesus said to him, "They have no wine." And Jesus said to her, "Woman, what concern is that to me and to you?"... His mother said to the servants, "Do whatever he tells you."... Jesus said to them, "Fill the jars with water." And they filled them up to the brim. He said to them, "Now draw some out, and take it to the person in charge of the banquet."... When

the person in charge tasted the water that had become wine and did not know where it came from, that person called the bridegroom and said to him, "Everyone serves the good wine first…but you have kept the good wine until now." (see John 2:2–10)

Jesus's compassionate, tolerant, and forgiving response during a dramatic encounter with a mob proves that, contrary to most people's belief, God is not judgmental and vengeful. Once, the scribes and Pharisees brought a woman who had been caught in adultery and made her stand before all of them. They said to Jesus,

"Teacher, this woman was caught in the very act of committing adultery. Now in the law Moses commanded us to stone such women. Now what do you say?"… When they kept on questioning him, he straightened up and said to them, "Let anyone among you who is without sin be the first to throw a stone at her."… When they heard it, they went away, one by one…. Jesus straightened up and said to her, "Woman, where are they? Has no one condemned you?" She said, "No one, sir." And Jesus said, "Neither do I condemn you." (see John 8:3–11)

If God is like Jesus, then this incident destroys forever the belief that our creator is wrathful and punitive.

Two interesting little incidents demonstrate how God regards babies and children. Once, the disciples asked,

"Who is the greatest in the kingdom of heaven?" [Jesus] called a child, whom he put among them, and said, "Truly I tell you, unless you change and become like children, you will never enter the kingdom of heaven. Whoever becomes humble like this child is greatest in the kingdom of heaven. Whoever welcomes one such child in my name welcomes me. If any of you cause one of these little ones who believe in me to sin, it would be better for you if a great millstone were fastened around your neck and you were drowned in the depth of the sea." (see Matt 18:1–6)

On another occasion the scriptures say, "Children were being brought to him in order that he might lay his hands on them and pray. The disciples spoke sternly to those who brought them, but Jesus said, 'Let the little children come to me, and do not stop them, for it is to such as these that the kingdom of heaven belongs.' And he laid his hands on them" (Matt 19:13–15). These responses nullify the doctrine of depravity.

The story of the lost sheep and the parable of the prodigal son both reveal a God who cares passionately, forgives totally, and restores dramatically. When the shepherd found his sheep, he was extremely happy. The scriptures say, "When he comes home, he calls together his friends and neighbors, saying to them, 'Rejoice with me, for I have found my lost sheep.' Just so, I tell you, there will be more joy in heaven over one sinner who repents than over ninety-nine righteous persons who need no repentance" (Luke 15:6–7).

The prodigal had wasted everything and was feeding hogs when he decided to go home.

> But while he was still far off, his father saw him and was filled with compassion; he ran and put his arms around him and kissed him. Then the son said to him, "Father, I have sinned against heaven and before you; I am no longer worthy to be called your son." But the father said to his slaves, "Quickly, bring out a robe—the best one—and put it on him; put a ring on his finger and sandals on his feet. And get the fatted calf and kill it, and let us eat and celebrate, for this son of mine was dead and is alive again; he was lost and is found!" And they began to celebrate. (Luke 15:20–24)

This story is an analogy of salvation, but it does not mention atonement or sacrifice or even repentance; rather, it emphasizes love and acceptance.

Jesus always expressed his feelings openly. At Lazarus's grave his empathy caused him to share in the family's grief. The scriptures say,

"Jesus began to weep" (John 11:35). This is more evidence that God has great concern for his people.

What kind of God do you believe in? This is a universal question. When Philip said, "Show us the Father, and we will be satisfied," Jesus replied, "You still do you not know me? Whoever has seen me has seen the Father" (see John 14:8–9). He was saying, "Look at my character, my attitudes, my words, and my actions and you will see an accurate reflection of God."

Most religions do not portray a God like Jesus. They proclaim he is critical of sinners and vindictive. Jesus wasn't! They imply God wants us to give him a lot of obeisance and praise. Jesus didn't! They insist that sacrifices must be made and someone must shed blood before God will forgive. Jesus never suggested such a thing.

Jesus came to demonstrate the true nature of God because he knew that trying to obey and worship an unknown God is both useless and destructive. Human beings need a God whose character, principles, and purposes can be discovered, understood, and emulated. This is crucial because nothing in our life can be right until our concept of God is right.

Jesus said, "If you know me, you will know my Father also" (John 14:7). If we believe this statement, then throughout his ministry Jesus has taught us that God loves all people—from innocent babies to convicted criminals, from rich kings to poor beggars, from the healthy to the sick and the lame and the blind. He invited people of all races and all nationalities, from the east, the west, the north, and the south.

Contrary to many popular stereotypes of religious figures, Jesus was a sensible person. He emphasized important issues like service and productivity while ignoring petty rules and regulations. Jesus also demonstrated God's great tolerance and mercy by actually forgiving those who were crucifying him. If he was revealing God's personal attributes, then surely such a creator must be concerned about hurting people. He must be interested in important matters, like helping needy men and women. He wouldn't be upset about trivial rules and regulations. He would be eager to accept and forgive everyone who comes to him. If God is like Jesus, then he can't be a vengeful tyrant who spends his time devising various means of punishment for heretics and setting up torture chambers for sinners.

It's fortunate that we can greatly increase our knowledge of God by analyzing Jesus's character and ministry.

Section 3

We Can Know God by Studying Scriptural Prophecy and Revelation

For millennia, people of all races and cultures have wondered about God. They have even attempted to worship God without much information about his character and requirements. Fortunately, in the scriptures we find a few special individuals who gained spiritual insights that can be helpful to us in our own personal search for God.

Abraham is often called the "father of a nation" (see Gen 17:4). The writer of Hebrews said, "By faith Abraham obeyed when he was called to set out for a place that he was to receive as an inheritance, and he set out, not knowing where he was going.... For he looked forward to the city that has foundations, whose architect and builder is God" (Heb 11:8, 10).

Abraham was willing to risk, to change, and to move from the status quo toward a better life. Later, he made a tremendous leap in religious beliefs and practices by realizing God did not require human sacrifice. Archaeologists have found evidence that this horrible custom was fairly common at that time. Abraham even considered it with his son Isaac, but at the last moment, he sensed God's voice telling him to stop. This momentous event, which prevented the Hebrews from performing such a pagan ritual in the future, is described this way:

> Abraham built an altar there and laid the wood in order. He bound his son Isaac and laid him on the altar on top of the wood. Then Abraham reached out his hand and took the knife to kill his son. But the angel of the LORD called to him from heaven and said, "Abraham, Abraham!"

> And he said, "Here I am." He said, "Do not lay your hand on the boy or do anything to him"... And Abraham looked up and saw a ram, caught in a thicket by its horns. Abraham went and took the ram and offered it up as a burnt offering instead of his son. (Gen. 22:9–12, 13)

The substitution of an animal was not a final and perfect solution, but it was a step in the right direction.

Abraham's faith and his ability to understand what is really required in worship adds to our knowledge about God. James said, "Abraham believed God, and it was reckoned to him as righteousness, and he was called the friend of God" (Jas 2:23).

Jacob also adds to our knowledge even though he seems to be an unlikely person for Christians to emulate. He deceived his father and cheated his brother, but he did have an affinity for God and was able to change. In spite of his flaws and weaknesses, he had a deep desire for spirituality, as revealed in his dreams: "He dreamed that there was a stairway set up on the earth, the top of it reaching to heaven, and the angels of God were ascending and descending on it. And the LORD stood beside him and said, 'I am the LORD.... The land on which you lie I will give to you and your offspring.... And all the families of the earth shall be blessed in you" (Gen 28:12–14).

Jacob was a determined and persistent individual. He had patience and worked hard for success. He loved deeply and spent long years overcoming serious obstacles to win Rachel's hand in marriage (see Gen 29:18–30).

Jacob's real epiphany came when he struggled all night to receive a blessing: "Jacob was left alone, and a man wrestled with him until daybreak.... Then he said, 'Let me go, for the day in breaking.' But Jacob said, 'I will not let you go, unless you bless me.' So he said to him, 'What is your name?' And he said, 'Jacob' Then the man said, 'You shall no longer be called Jacob, but Israel, for you have striven with God and with humans and have prevailed.'... And there he blessed him" (Gen 32:24, 26–28, 29).

Jacob's experience shows us that God deals with and even blesses sinful individuals if they are willing to change.

Joseph is another interesting and unusual character. He began life as a spoiled kid who alienated his siblings. It was only after being sold into slavery, being convicted of a crime he didn't commit, and spending time in prison that he changed. His integrity and wisdom enabled him to become a high-ranking official in Egypt. When his family became desperate for food and traveled there for help, his response was compassionate and kind.

Joseph was able to exemplify several godly traits, but the most important one was forgiveness: "Joseph could no longer control himself before all those who stood by him, and he cried out, 'Send everyone away from me.' So no one stayed with him when Joseph made himself known to his brothers. And he wept so loudly that the Egyptians heard it, and the household of Pharaoh heard it. Joseph said to his brothers, 'I am Joseph. Is my father still alive?' But his brothers could not answer him, so dismayed were they at his presence" (Gen 45:1–3).

Then Joseph explained how God can turn evil into good, saying, "I am your brother, Joseph, whom you sold into Egypt. And now do not be distressed or angry with yourselves because you sold me here, for God sent me before you to preserve life. For the famine has been in the land these two years, and there are five more years in which there will be neither plowing nor harvest. God sent me before you to preserve for you a remnant on earth and to keep alive for you many survivors. So it was not you who sent me here but God" (Gen 45:4–8). This mature assessment showed that Joseph had a depth of understanding and spiritual insight. In the New Testament, Paul teaches this same doctrine: "All things work together for good to those who love God" (Rom 8:28).

Most people are aware that Moses became a great leader of the Israelites, taking them from Egypt toward the promised land. He had more education than the typical Hebrew because he had been adopted by the daughter of Pharaoh. His major contribution to religion was his emphasis on ethical standards. He was able to write and codify social rules and give us the Ten Commandments (see Exod 34:27–28). These laws did not exemplify the highest principles of spirituality, but they were certainly another step toward lifting the worship of God from a system of bribery and sacrifice to a system of moral choices and good behavior. As a result, Moses was able to identify the Hebrew religion with righteousness and justice.

David is a popular Bible story hero. This multitalented and passionate individual was a military leader, a gifted musician, and a deeply spiritual person. His songs and psalms reveal unusual personal honesty and empathy. He did have faults, and he did commit sins, but he always admitted them.

One of David's prayers is a classic example of sincere repentance:

> Wash me thoroughly from my iniquity, and cleanse me from my sin. For I know my transgressions, and my sin is ever before me.... You desire truth in the inward being; therefore teach me wisdom in my secret heart. Purge me with hyssop, and I shall be clean; wash me, and I shall be whiter than snow.... Create in me a clean heart, O God, and put a new and right spirit within me. Do not cast me away from your presence, and do not take your holy spirit from me. Restore to me the joy of your salvation. (Ps 51:2–3, 6–7, 10–12)

David had definitely progressed past the common belief that God could be persuaded by sacrificial bribes. He understood God's nature better than most of his associates: "You have no delight in sacrifice; if I were to give a burnt offering, you would not be pleased. The sacrifice acceptable to God is a broken spirit; a broken and contrite heart, O God, you will not despise" (Ps 51:16–17).

When we think of David, most of us remember that he killed Goliath, but his authentic personality, sincere emotional expressions, and profound insights are much more important. These traits are what caused God to say, "I have found David, son of Jesse, to be a man after my heart, who will carry out all my wishes" (Acts 13:22).

After David and Solomon the scriptures introduce many major and minor prophets who were developing theology and gradually adding to our knowledge of God. One of the greatest, Isaiah, didn't come out of the wilderness as an angry fanatic full of denunciations. He was cultured and well-educated. He used diplomatic language and associated with people from every level of society—from beggars and thieves to leaders and rulers.

Once, Isaiah had a disturbing vision in the temple. He explained his experience, saying, "I saw the LORD sitting on a throne.... I said, 'Woe is me!... My eyes have seen the King.'... Then one of the seraphs flew to me, holding a live coal.... The seraph touched my mouth with it and said, 'Now that this has touched your lips, your guilt has departed and your sin is blotted out" (see Isa 6:1–7).

Traditionally, seeing or touching a holy thing was thought to be fatal. This is the first reference of a person who did so and lived. Instead of dying, Isaiah felt cleansed as the burning coal touched his lips. When he sensed the Lord asking, "Whom shall I send, and who will go for us?" his immediate response was, "Here am I; send me!" (Isa 6:8). As a result of this experience, Isaiah changed the word *holiness*, with its implication of terror, into a term meaning purity and righteousness.

Isaiah also gave the word *spirit* a new meaning. It originally meant nothing more than wind, with no religious connotation. But Jesus quotes Isaiah, saying, "The Spirit of the Lord is upon me, because he has anointed me to bring good news to the poor" (Luke 4:18).

The multitudes, delayed by old taboos and inherited superstitions, always lagged far behind the prophets. These theologians and philosophers typified the highest and best in religious thinking. They had begun to have an inner consciousness of a personal God, who did not require them to go through sacrifices or priestly offices.

Another great prophet, Jeremiah, represents a real turning point in spiritual history. As a questioner and a doubter, he was a pioneer in the liberation of conscience. His own painful experiences forced him to develop a profoundly deeper religion. Because he refused to rationalize and meekly accept traditional doctrines, Jeremiah actually saved Israel theologically but was branded as a traitor for advocating compromise. People who hold "middle of the road" positions are often despised because extremism is more dramatic and emotionally satisfying. They burned his books and threatened his life; but that didn't nullify his thoughts. His commitment transcended their narrow views. He was beginning to envision a wider world.

This man of priestly descent lived through the trying times of exile, persecution, and the destruction of many religious traditions. He was a sensitive, serious, and dedicated loner from his youth. Many ordinary life pleasures were denied him because of his calling. The fact that he never married and had children disproved the common belief that immortality was achieved only through heirs. It also demonstrated that individual worth could be had apart from procreation, family, and clan.

As a young man Jeremiah had been an orthodox member of the current prophetic movement. At first his beliefs were similar to those of the other theologians. Fortunately, his clear foresight soon outran their superficiality. He is the perfect example of one who was able to grow and move beyond his group.

To Jeremiah the old formula of retribution and punishment for disobedience seemed to fit the public situation, since the national sins were horrendous, but his own personal grief was an enigma. As a result, he began to look at others who hurt and was much too honest to ignore what he saw. He, like Job, saw the wicked escaping penalty and the innocent enduring tragedy. Out of his protests and explorations came great forward movement.

Jeremiah had the thankless task of a reforming critic. He could not condone the evil actions that others around him were willing to accept. He insisted people couldn't steal, lie, commit adultery, and burn incense to idols and then say, "We're safe because we're in God's house" (see Jer 7:8–10).

His views were beginning to differ greatly from the other religious leaders, and as usual this was resented! He raised hard questions, and out of his experiences were born the most valid principles of Judaism. His doctrine of the individual relating to God as a person, not as a Jew, was an original and significant insight.

Jeremiah's demand for a thorough conversion of the inner self also broke new ground. He felt a personal identity with God and believed his life had a purpose. Jeremiah's call was direct: "The LORD put out his hand and touched my mouth" (Jer 1:9). This was a great change from the fearsome God that Moses had depicted.

Jeremiah was a unique individual. He never lost his personality in his message. The authentic man comes through. Of course, his ideas offended many traditionalists. He questioned the paradox of the affluent wicked. He argued with God. He even accused God of abandoning Israel.

He wasn't always reverent, and his language was often far from sacred, but he was real, and he was honest.

The people of Israel rejected Jeremiah's ideas and accused him of heresy, but his theology prevailed. Jeremiah perceived that it takes transformed people to make a transformed nation. He was the first to quote God as saying, "I will put my law within them, and I will write it on their hearts" (Jer 31:33).

The prophet Ezekiel was also among the captives taken during the exile. He saw the nation's sins and with earnest, almost fanatical zeal called for genuine repentance.

Ezekiel's most important insight is that individuals will be held accountable for their own behavior. Over the centuries, the Jews had taught and believed that whole tribes were punished for the sins of one person. The prophets kept bringing up the sins of past generations to add to the guilt of the present. The people were starting to say, "The parents have eaten sour grapes, and the children's teeth are set on edge" (Ezek 18:2). In other words, "If we must keep paying for the past, what's the use of trying?" The old doctrine of retribution was killing their spirit.

Individualism led to a whole new ethical concept. Ezekiel quoted God as saying, "All lives are mine; the life of the parent as well as the life of the child is mine: it is only the person who sins that shall die" (Ezek 18:4). This prophet believed individuals are responsible before God for their own behavior, unaffected by what others may have done. No one is tied to his past. Each child is born free of inherited guilt. In other words, they aren't burdened with original sin. They build their own character and determine their own destiny.

Ezekiel also emphasized the new idea that every person is called by God to perform the duty of a watchman on behalf of his friends and associates. He believed God had said, "I have made you a sentinel for the house of Israel; whenever you hear a word from my mouth, you shall give them warning from me" (Ezek 3:17).

Another prophet, Hosea, was a peasant whose perceptions and insights came from his own bitter experience. It took the emotional upheaval of a tragic marriage to break the traditional mindset about a wrathful God. Through his own grief and undying love for the faithless Gomer, he began to realize that God can continue to love a faithless Israel. He rejected a vindictive deity and was able to hate sin without hating the sinner.

Hosea saw that behind divine wrath lay an unquenchable compassion. Other prophets thundered of God's power and wrath. Hosea whispered of God's love and mercy. He believed that for both Gomer and Israel, the door of hope was always open.

The sorrow of Hosea's family life gave depth and reality to his message. His inability to cease loving a wife who had forfeited all rights to such love seemed inexplicable on a natural basis. Therefore, the idea began to filter through that such unconditional love and unmerited grace must be of God.

Joel was a minor prophet who made one major contribution to theology. He realized that the future would be more progressive and would involve more people. He saw a time when prejudice in the areas of gender, age, and social class would be abolished and quotes God as saying, "Afterward I will pour out my spirit on all flesh; your sons and your daughters will prophesy, your old men shall dream dreams, and your young men shall see visions. Even on the male and female slaves, in those days I will pour out my spirit" (Joel 2:28–29). His positive, enlightened views were repeated by Peter on the day of Pentecost (see Acts 2:17–18). This should influence our attitudes about gender bias in the twenty-first century.

Amos was a farmer whose ideas about the creator had developed far beyond the war God concept of Moses's era. He certainly didn't expect God to head Israel's army and send fire and brimstone on her enemies. Nationally, there was great expectation for the "day of the Lord," when Israel would rule the world. Amos saw instead a day of judgment. He held out hope only for the spiritually minded and morally pure. He questioned the commandments concerning ceremonies and described God as despising hypocritical offerings, feasts, and sacrifices. If God is wise and righteous, then we know the morality of his worshipers would be much more important to him than the observance of correct rituals.

Amos quotes God as saying, "I hate, I despise your festivals, and I take no delight in your solemn assemblies. Even though you offer me your burnt offerings and grain offerings, I will not accept them, and the offerings of well-being of your fatted animals I will not look upon.

Take away from me the noise of your songs; I will not listen to the melody of your harps. But let justice roll down like water and righteousness like an ever-flowing stream" (Amos 5:21–24). This clear declaration proves that religious ceremonies and empty worship practices are irrelevant to God. A thousand perfect sheep sacrificed on a thousand holy altars, and ten thousand rivers of sacred oil mingled with ten thousand oblations are nothing, but one good thought, one encouraging word, or one merciful deed is of eternal significance. Correct ceremonies, proper words, and complicated sacraments are nothing, but positive attitudes and loving concern are of extreme significance.

Micah reinforced the prophecies of both Hosea and Amos. His searching questions threw light on what was authentic. His crusade for social justice condemned violence, unfair courts, and greedy nobles who seized land from helpless peasants.

Sacrifices were still considered a crucial element in Israel's tradition, but Micah denied their importance. He saw clearly that animal offerings furnished no true way of approaching God. His inquiry into what God really wants from people revealed great progressive insight. Desperate people were anxious to know what forms of service were acceptable, asking, "What shall we do to appease God? Wherewith shall I come before the Lord? Shall I come before him with burnt offerings, with calves of a year old?" In the past these acts had been considered sufficient, but now the worshipers realize more was required. They pled, "Will the Lord be pleased with thousands of rams, or with ten thousands of rivers of oil?" Of course, these exaggerations are absurd and were only used to show that all such things are futile.

Finally, one terrible possibility remains. The people reluctantly asked, "Shall I give my firstborn for my transgression, the fruit of my body for the sin of my soul?" (Micah 6:7). In this ultimate overture they are saying, "Shall we return to the human sacrifices our ancestors practiced?" Of course this is unthinkable!

After their last cry of agony Micah became empathetic. He saw the people's sincere desire for God and understood that even behind the abominable idea of child sacrifice lay the motive of trying to give the best to their creator. His profound answer to their questions ignored the traditional rituals that had been required. Instead, it included fundamental spiritual qualities. He was able to express the essence of religion in one single phrase: "To do justice, and to love kindness and to walk humbly with your God" (Micah 6:8). He rightly concluded that such a principle, put into practice on an individual basis, would result in world peace. He said, "They shall beat their swords into plowshares and their spears into pruning hooks; nation shall not lift up sword against nation; neither shall they learn war any more" (Micah 4:3). Micah's real message and contribution was the firm belief that God cared much more for right attitudes and actions than he did for holy places and pedantic ceremonies.

Another prophet, Habakkuk, voiced the ever-present cry that we still hear today: "Why does evil go unpunished?" His questions and doubts were especially poignant. He was vainly trying to make the old platitudes work, and yet was honorable enough to admit that they didn't. His basic thesis concerned the strength of evil compared to the worth of good. He implied that a man is not measured by his outward status or material possessions, but by his spiritual integrity.

Habakkuk refuted the common belief that religion will pay off in success and earthly rewards. In an eloquent expression he said, "Though the fig tree does not blossom and no fruit is on the vines; though the produce of the olive fails and the fields yield no food; though the flock is cut off from the fold and there is no herd in the stalls, yet I will rejoice in the LORD; I will exult in the God of my salvation. GOD, the Lord, is my strength; he makes my feet like the feet of a deer and makes me tread upon the heights" (Hab 3:17–19).

Habakkuk would not be attracted to the prosperity gospel that is being promoted in some congregations today. Instead, he majored on central truths and took the long view that evil always fails in the end, even though it may seem to succeed for the moment.

In the New Testament, growth continued. Jesus's disciple, Simon Peter, was a complex person, both uncouth and wise, both rebellious and loyal. He denied Jesus but was willing to die for him. Jesus recognized and dealt with his volatile personality. Once, he complimented Peter by saying, "Blessed are you, Simon son of Jonah!" (Matt 16:17), and then a short time later he scolded Peter by saying, "Get behind me, Satan!" (Matt 16:23).

Like all of us, Peter had both high and low moments, but he was teachable, and he grew socially and spiritually. We know that this man, who had once been rude and bigoted, was finally able to say, "I truly understand that God shows no partiality" (Acts 10:34).

John was another disciple who had deep spiritual discernment. In fact, he identified so closely with the Lord that he was known as "that one whom Jesus loved." He grasped the Christian's role in the world better than most of us have even today, saying, "As he is, so are we in this world" (1 John 4:17).

Paul is a biblical writer who reveals many attributes of God. He had been a fanatical Pharisee who persecuted and killed early Christians and tried to destroy new congregations. Then, an event on the road to Damascus dramatically changed his life (see Acts 22:1–15).

Paul wrote much of the New Testament and served as a missionary for many years. But his greatest contribution to the Christian gospel was the concept of grace. He had experienced such an enormous sense of relief when he finally understood the gospel that it became his life theme: "Since we are justified by faith, we have peace with God through our Lord Jesus Christ, through whom we have obtained access to this grace in which we stand" (Rom 5:1–2). In giving his testimony about a personal problem, he said, "Three times I appealed to the Lord about this, that it would leave me, but he said to me, 'My grace is sufficient for you'" (2 Cor 12:9).

To Paul, grace meant there were no more sacrifices, no more pedantic laws, no more worry over keeping the rules, no more guilt, and no more fear of punishment! To Paul this was indeed a miracle, and he couldn't wait to share it with the world.

All these prophets and writers and disciples learned, matured, and shared their ideas about God, but we're still limited. An inadequate vocabulary and language difficulties add to our problems. The definition of words and changes in their meaning also cause misunderstanding. For instance, the word *lost* does not mean evil, depraved, or rebellious. Rather, it suggests confusion and disorientation. People who are alienated from their support group, with no clear sense of direction, are to be helped, not criticized and condemned. Then, when the scriptures say we are to fear God, the word translated *fear* usually means to revere or to respect.

We know Jesus does not want us to be afraid of God, because in the same passage that he advises us to "fear the one…who has authority to cast into hell," he also says, "Do not be afraid" (see Luke 12:5–7). John goes even further, saying, "There is no fear in love, but perfect love casts out fear; for fear has to do with punishment, and whoever fears has not reached perfection in love" (1 John 4:18).

Other terms in religious vocabulary are confusing to people. For instance, the word *justify* is not an artificial pronouncement of innocence. God doesn't say, "You are really guilty and depraved, but because you believe Jesus paid your penalty, I now declare you to be righteous." That would be deceitful and ludicrous. Instead, he says, "Since you were created in my image, you have divine worth. So begin to live like that. Don't let anyone accuse and condemn you." We also know salvation is a real psychological change rather than some strange, magical metamorphosis.

In his wonderful parables of the coin, the sheep, and the son, Jesus pictures three striking characteristics of those who are lost. The coin, lying hidden in the dust, is useless. The sheep, huddled alone in the wilderness, is afraid. The son, starving in a pig pen, is miserable. Jesus portrays a compassionate and caring heavenly Father who tirelessly seeks those who need to be redeemed and then gives them purpose, peace, and joy.

Redemption remakes that which has been damaged and scarred. Once, a cathedral was noted for a large stained-glass window behind its altar. Unfortunately, one night, a storm shattered it into a thousand pieces. These scraps were put into a box and stored in the basement. One day, a stranger asked if he could have the fragments. Since they seemed totally worthless, the custodian gave him permission to take them. A year later, that custodian was invited to an art show in a nearby village. When the artist unveiled his work, it was a masterpiece, created from those pieces of splintered glass from the original window. Surprisingly, it was far more beautiful than before. Likewise, God is a reclaimer of worthless misfits, a recoverer of broken lives, and a restorer of shattered personalities. The life restored is always more beautiful than it was before.

When we find a piece of driftwood and turn it into a lamp, we are salvaging. When we dive under the menacing waves of a dark sea to bring a tarnished treasure up into the sunlight, we are salvaging. When we snatch a valuable piece of art from a raging fire, we are salvaging. Jesus was a specialist in the salvaging business. He took miserable prostitutes, crooked tax collectors, and uncouth fishermen and turned them into saints.

Most people and most religions also misunderstand ideas of a wrathful God and eternal punishment. We know now that a reasonable, loving God doesn't have temper tantrums and impose cruel punishments on everyone who breaks a rule or makes a mistake. Furthermore, if God wanted to use a sinner's death as a lesson, he certainly wouldn't resort to torture. People today believe that even the vilest criminal should be executed by humane methods. Surely imperfect human beings aren't more compassionate than a God of love!

Consequences and punishments do have shaping purposes. But God isn't vengeful. God doesn't retaliate. Rather, God teaches. Lord Halifax said, "Men are not hanged for stealing horses. Rather they are hanged so that horses will not be stolen." Our legal system should be for the purpose of ensuring good behavior, not merely for the purpose of imposing after-the-fact pain.

Likewise, if judgment is reserved for the "day of the Lord," it will be too late. If punishment is delayed until we reach the "great white throne," it will be useless. At that time any of its value as a deterrent will have been nullified, and only vengeance will remain. That's unthinkable! We can only learn from our mistakes and be motivated by the penalties if the cause-and-effect chain is activated in the earthly present rather than in the heavenly future.

Christians need to understand God's methods and know God's will. We need to develop a relationship with him to enjoy his fellowship. We need to establish a partnership with him to care for his natural resources.

There is an old joke about a farmer sitting on his porch, looking out over the well-kept fields and neatly painted fences. He and his family had worked hard over the years to develop the place.

A neighbor said, "This sure is beautiful. You and the Lord have done a real good job here in this wilderness."

The farmer answered, "Yeah, I guess that's right. But man, you ought to have seen it when the Lord had it all by himself!"

That's true, but God doesn't have it all by himself. He provides the resources, but we are responsible for managing and utilizing them. He doesn't do our job.

It's also reassuring to know God doesn't deal in generalities. A doctor doesn't come into his crowded waiting room and give a public lecture on health rules. Instead, he sees, diagnoses, and prescribes for each patient on an individual basis. Likewise, an intimate, personal God deals individually with his people.

When one of Queen Victoria's maids lost her husband in a tragic accident, the queen removed her crown and royal robes, dressed in a plain shawl, and had her footman drive her to the grieving widow's home. As the carriage stopped, the woman approached and bowed in deference. The queen immediately lifted her up and said, "No! Today I do not come to you as monarch to subject. Today I come to you as friend to friend!" That is the essence of God's covenant relationship, which began with Abraham. The scripture says, "[Abraham] was called the friend of God" (Jas 2:23).

Jesus picked up on the same theme when he said, "I do not call you servants any longer.... I have called you friends" (John 15:15). This is the highest offer God can make, the greatest compliment he can bestow.

Once, a boarding school had a strict rule that if any boy made noise after "lights out," he would have to take his bedroll and spend the night in an isolated storage room.

The inevitable happened. The headmaster, making evening inspections, found the smallest and shyest student throwing a pillow. The rule was a rule! The scared, homesick little boy began to cry and begged for leniency. "Couldn't I get by just this once?" he pleaded. "After all, it was my first offense. Couldn't you just overlook it? Couldn't you change the penalty?"

The headmaster said, "No, I'm very sorry, but you and I both agreed to abide by this school's code when we came here. If I let you off, if I made one exception, I'd undermine the institution's credibility. I'd destroy my own integrity. I'd lose the respect of the other students. You broke the rule; you must pay the price."

As the child slowly and fearfully began to drag his blanket toward the dreaded place of punishment, the teacher said something else: "It's true! I can't undo the deed. I can't turn back the clock. I can't abolish the consequences, but there is something I can do. I can go with you. There's nothing in the rules to prevent me from sleeping beside you." God is like that!

David said, "Yea, though I walk through the valley of the shadow of death, I will fear no evil: for thou art with me" (Ps 23:4 KJV). Jesus verifies this by saying, "I am with you always, to the end of the age" (Matt 28:20).

So how can we know God? The scripture says, "The LORD gives wisdom; from his mouth come knowledge and understanding" (Prov 2:6).

The deepest thinkers and the best minds of every race and nation have spent lifetimes seeking God. Every religion, every ideology, and every cult has created some idea of God and some form of worship. Trying to separate the false from the true, the idols from the divine spirit, is difficult. Every group develops its own image for reverence, its own set of rules and requirements, its own list of taboos and restrictions, and its own liturgies and ceremonies.

There's a downside to this situation. Having so many different belief systems and worship practices causes chaos and confrontation. This leads to riots, crusades, and even wars as each worshiper fanatically proclaims his doctrinal views.

But there is also an upside to the development of so many religions. It shows human beings are deeply concerned about spiritual things. They are reaching out and looking up. They are seeking better beliefs and more perfect role models.

Because of these serious prophets and researchers, there are a few general principles that are beginning to have worldwide acceptance and agreement. Reverence for life is practically a universal axiom. Fairness is now seen as a fundamental right by most groups. Freedom is also a basic aspiration shared by people everywhere. God isn't autocratic or dogmatic. He gives us free will. He doesn't change. He is dependable.

If the concept of God can attract so much interest and attention by so many seekers for so many centuries, he can't be just a figment of the imagination or a temporary fad to be casually dismissed. Since the need for God, the desire for God, and the search for God is universal, such a creator must be a righteous, consistent, and consequential being that we can depend on and emulate.

It's fortunate we can learn how God has dealt with his people over the years by studying scriptural prophecy and revelation.

Section 4

We Can Know God by Experiencing Human Love and Companionship

God has always expected people to interact with each other. Most individuals get their first ideas about God from their parents, their Sunday school teachers, and their ministers and priests. Even in the Old Testament, fathers were told to teach their children about God. The scriptures say,

> Take care and watch yourselves closely, so as neither to forget the things that your eyes have seen nor to let them slip from your mind all the days of your life; make them known to your children and your children's children—how you once stood before the LORD your God at Horeb, when the LORD said to me, "Assemble the people for me, and I will let them hear my words, so that they may learn to fear me as long as they live on the earth and may teach their children so. (see Deut 4:9–10)

The psalmist said, "Come, O children, listen to me; I will teach you the fear of the LORD" (Ps 34:11).

Even so, each person seems to have a different concept of God. Since we call God "our Father," men and women who have a good relationship with their own fathers usually have a positive view of God. But those who have problems with their fathers, those who were abused or abandoned by their fathers, and those who never knew their fathers may have negative or warped views about God. Then, all these varying views of God will be passed on to others. Everybody assumes that what they've heard all their lives or what they've been told in church or seen on television is the truth about God, but many of these things are based on faulty evidence. Very little of this material includes verified information. Instead, it simply reflects the opinions of other people. We need firsthand knowledge and logical facts. Two thousand years ago, seekers could approach Jesus to find out about God, but we can't do that. We must do our own research. We must form our own beliefs. We must decide for ourselves.

Of course, all of us are influenced by other people. In the New Testament, Andrew brought his brother, Peter, to Jesus. The scriptures say,

> The next day John again was standing with two of his disciples, and as he watched Jesus walk by he exclaimed, "Look, here is the Lamb of God!" The two disciples heard him say this, and they followed Jesus. When Jesus turned and saw them following, he said to them, "What are you looking for?" They said to him, "Rabbi" (which translated means Teacher), "where are you staying?" He said to them, "Come and see." They came and saw where he was staying, and they remained with him that day. It was about four o'clock in the afternoon. One of the two who heard John speak and followed him was Andrew, Simon Peter's brother. He first found his brother Simon and said to him, "We have found the Messiah" (which is translated Anointed). He brought Simon[b] to Jesus, who looked at him and said, "You are Simon son of John. You are to be called Cephas" (which is translated Peter). (see John 1:35–42)

On another occasion, both Philip and Andrew brought some questioning Greeks to Jesus. The scriptures say, "Now among those who went up to worship at the festival were some Greeks. They came to Philip…and said to him, 'Sir, we wish to see Jesus.' Philip went and told Andrew, then Andrew and Philip went and told Jesus" (John 12:20–22).

Later, we discover that the Philippian jailer who was converted influenced his entire family. The scriptures say, "The jailer called for lights, and rushing in, he fell down trembling before Paul and Silas. Then he brought them outside and said, 'Sirs, what must I do to be saved?'

They answered, 'Believe in the Lord Jesus, and you will be saved, you and your household.' They spoke the word of the Lord to him and to all who were in his house. At the same hour of the night he took them and washed their wounds; then he and his entire family were baptized without delay" (Acts 16:29–33).

People have always expressed their religious beliefs to those around them. People have always shared their faith with friends and associates. People have always witnessed to others through their words and actions. Over the years, there could be an honor roll of the names of the great evangelists, artists, musicians, authors, poets, and educators who have influenced not only their neighbors, but entire nations and indeed the world. We've learned about God from the art, music, books, poems, and other contributions of these gifted ones. Then there are the heroes, like David Livingstone, Albert Schweitzer, and Mother Teresa, who spent their lives in the service of humanity.

Many faithful martyrs like Joan of Arc, Gandhi, and Martin Luther King Jr. were killed because of their religious beliefs, their scientific discoveries, or their loyalty to their country or cause. These courageous individuals have benefited many lives and changed the destinies of cultural groups, institutions, and civilizations. We can also see the godlike traits of compassion and concern shown by police officers, firefighters, and military personnel who put their lives on the line every day for both their fellow citizens and foreigners.

Finally, there are ordinary people who give blood and donate organs to their neighbors and even to strangers. Many individuals are willing to save a baby from a burning building or pull a drowning woman from a flooded car. There are also benefactors who give scholarships and philanthropists who endow hospitals and surgeons who donate their services in poverty areas. All these people are demonstrating God's love for us.

We can learn about divine attributes by observing the generosity of countless unnamed, unidentified, and unknown men and women who work hard doing thankless tasks, healing the sick, feeding the hungry, caring for the forgotten, and saving lives. We can observe the overwhelming expressions of empathy and support that always come after tragedies such as hurricanes or mass shootings. In fact, it's the positive characteristics and loving relationships of people that identify them as Christians.

It's important to note that real heroes do not glorify themselves or emphasize their importance. They know that sometimes we must be willing to diminish our own significance to serve. That's why Jesus describes us as leaven, salt, and light. We never exclaim "Oh, what wonderful yeast" when we take a bite of bread; "What yummy salt" when we eat a baked potato; "What glorious light" when we read by an electric lamp. Each of these items quietly sacrifices its own distinctiveness to accomplish a greater good and serve a larger purpose.

There's an old legend that describes how much faith Jesus had in his followers and future believers. When he returned to heaven, he explained about his time on earth—his ministry and his hopes for the coming of the kingdom. One of the angels who listened to his plans said, "Master, your message about God was wonderful, but how will these teachings continue now that you are no longer there?"

Jesus answered, "I told the few followers I had to tell others and for them to continue telling others until everyone will know."

"Oh," the angel said. "But, sir, what if they don't do that? What if they forget?"

Jesus replied, "Then my sacrifice was in vain. I have no other plan."

A person-to-person communication system has always been the plan. Paul says, "You yourselves are our letter, written on our hearts, known and read by all, and you show that you are a letter of Christ, prepared by us, written not with ink but with the Spirit of the living God, not on tablets of stone but on tablets that are human hearts" (2 Cor 3:2–3).

Christians are not supposed to emulate the attitudes of those around them. Instead, they are to influence those attitudes in positive ways. If you carry a lamp into a dim, shadowy room, you certainly don't turn your light down to imitate your surroundings. Rather, you turn it up to compensate for the darkness. Likewise, Christians involved in negative, hostile situations must not "follow the leader" and turn their own love lights down. They should do the opposite. They should turn their love lights up to compensate for the spiritual darkness around them.

In a fable, the sun overheard some animals discussing darkness. They talked of the terror of black caves and deep forests where no light penetrated. "I don't understand," the sun thought. "I'll go see for myself." So he went to all the places they had mentioned and found that they were not dark at all, but rather brilliantly illuminated. "They're mistaken about darkness," the sun concluded. "There is no such place." He was right. There was no such place for him, because his light was within. He carried it wherever he went.

There is a lot of spiritual darkness in our world today, and when Christians are trying to worship a false god, or a misunderstood God, or an unknown God, they are at a tremendous disadvantage. Their message is contaminated, and their witness is compromised.

Sometimes we waste our lives over things that don't matter. A little old lady, on her first airplane trip, fussed with her parcels, pillows, and wraps. Consequently, she missed all the sights. Later, she wailed, "Oh, my! If I'd known the trip was going to be so short, I wouldn't have wasted my time on trifles."

Life, also, is too short to waste on trifles.

Different people have different priorities. Each individual tends to notice and deal with specific things and ignore other things. Both vultures and hummingbirds fly over the California deserts. The vultures see only rotten meat, because that's all they look for. Hummingbirds, on the other hand, ignore the carcasses and look for the fragrant cactus flowers. Each bird finds what it looks for. As Christians we also find what we look for.

Too many people are satisfied with a limited life. They don't take advantage of the opportunities and freedom God offers. A tourist out West stopped at a service station. While his tank was being filled, he noticed a dejected eagle sitting in a small, dingy cage. "Would you sell that bird?" he asked the owner.

"I don't know," he replied. "Lots of folks like to see a genuine eagle."

The tourist finally prevailed by giving the man quite a bit of money. Then he walked over to the cage and opened the door.

"Be careful," the startled manager shouted. "He'll escape!"

"I want him to escape," the purchaser retorted. "Eagles weren't meant for cages. They were meant to be free."

The bird flapped his majestic wings and soared proudly into the sky.

Human beings weren't made for cages either. They were made to be free. God doesn't want obedient robots or dutiful slaves. God rewards people who think for themselves, who question life's mysteries, and who analyze events. He wants individuals to find answers and discover solutions. God doesn't forbid doubts or punish rebellion. He knows that knowledge will set us free. If we can find the reasons behind a doctrine or a commandment, then we can understand and learn how to make our own decisions instead of merely submitting to authority.

For instance, reasonable people do not claim that something becomes right or wrong just because God or some authority figure says so. Instead, the very opposite is true. A wise God or a caring parent says so because these things are innately right and constructive or wrong and destructive. There's a tremendous moral difference between these two viewpoints.

Suppose a mother has apples and oranges at her disposal and a three-year-old asks for an apple. The mom might say, "No! You can have the orange, but not the apple."

"Why?"

"Because I said so!"

There doesn't seem to be a logical reason behind this edict. The adult is merely using her authority to impose her will. Obedience under such irrational circumstances will eventually turn into resentment.

If, on the other hand, there is a bottle of apple juice and a bottle of bleach and the three-year old wants to drink the bleach, the parent must say, "No! You can have the juice but not the bleach. It'll hurt you!" Now, there is a logical reason. The child may not totally understand the difference at the moment, but as he matures, he will begin to see that there are reasons behind his parents' prohibitions, and he will not feel resentful.

It's the same with us! The better we know God and the more we understand the purposes behind his teachings and commandments, the more likely we'll be to make the best decisions with a positive attitude.

Jesus knew that our relationships with God and each other are very important. He said, "Everyone will know that you are my disciples, if you have love for one another" (John 13:35). He also said, "Let your light shine before others, so that they may see your good works and give glory to your Father in heaven" (Matt. 5:16). This scripture tells us that our behavior can glorify God by reflecting his traits and characteristics. This is both an enormous responsibility and a great honor. We've learned a lot over the years from theologians and heroes. We've also learned by observing ordinary men and woman who help others and pay forward their blessings.

There is evidence that as a civilization we are gradually becoming more humane and more benevolent. Some of the worst atrocities and the cruelest entertainments have been outlawed. Torture is forbidden in most nations. Slavery is no longer condoned, and capital punishment is no longer a public spectacle in most countries. There are also many more government agencies and benevolent charities available now to support needy people. Surely, if our creator's protective, compassionate, and generous traits can be observed in the lives of people around us, then he is a relevant, beneficial force and worthy of our respect and worship.

It's fortunate that we can see evidence of God's concern for us by experiencing human love and companionship.

Section 5

We Can Know God by Developing Our Own Personal Intuition and Insight

The Holy Spirit helps us rely on our own personal intuition. The Holy Spirit increases our reasoning and discernment skills. The Holy spirit encourages us to express our own insights. But in order to utilize this wonderful resource, we must abolish the common notion that this Spirit is some supernatural, external creature. We must understand that the Holy Spirit is a natural, internal enabler. This Spirit works through our own subconscious urges and our own intellectual faculties. It sharpens our memory and guides us in making decisions.

Of course, the Holy Spirit can only help us if we are willing to learn, open to new knowledge, and free to respond. That's why stifling thought, censoring speech, and banning experimentation are crimes against the soul. Yet that's what many religions have done!

In the very beginning, God said, "Let us make humans in our image, according to our likeness, and let them have dominion over the fish of the sea and over the birds of the air and over the cattle and over all the wild animals of the earth…. So God created humans in his image, in the image of God he created them; male and female he created them. God blessed them" (Gen 1:26–28).

This scripture says human beings are imaged after their creator. If so, then everyone shares the attributes of his maker. Indeed, if humanity had no commonality with God, the incarnation could not have occurred. If men and women have no spiritual dimension or no divine potential, then it would have been impossible for God to be reflected in the person of Jesus Christ. Yet he was!

Jesus described himself as the Son of Man. This phrase means one who fully exemplifies the qualities of ordinary human beings. Therefore, Jesus was truly one of us. He revealed the human personality as it was meant to be. He repudiated our self-contempt and demolished our guilt. He emphasized that we are free, autonomous, and valuable. Paul agreed with this: "You are no longer a slave but a child, and if a child then also an heir through God" (Gal 4:7). Every characteristic of God was exemplified by Jesus, and every characteristic of Jesus should be exemplified in each of us.

John's theme of spiritual oneness also expresses this idea (see John 17:11–21). Paul's teaching concerning the Christ in me reiterates this theme (see Gal 2:20). Many of us are still stuck at the God-in-him level, insisting that Jesus is the one and only incarnate manifestation of God. We refuse to regard him the way Paul does, as simply the "firstborn within a large family" (Rom 8:29). He is the unique model or prototype who came to prove that God can be incarnate in any human being who will think God's thoughts, speak God's words, and do God's works. Jesus himself prayed, "The glory that you have given me I have given them, so that they may be one, as we are one" (John 17:22).

This concept has not been emphasized by most religions. It's profound! It's almost beyond our ability to comprehend, but it's true. That's why, when Jesus realized his time here on earth was limited, he began considering how his life-giving message and special insights could still be expressed after his earthly departure. He realized there would be new problems and more questions in the future. He knew his followers would need information he could not give them at that time. He clearly revealed his concern about this when he said, "I still have many things to say to you, but you cannot bear them now" (John 16:12).

After considering the dilemma, he explained the idea of the Holy Spirit and promised his believers that if they were authentic and honest, they would be able to continue receiving wisdom and assistance directly from God. Even so, the subject of the Holy Spirit has never been fully understood. False teachings have caused superstition and unrealistic notions. Some beliefs have led to divisiveness and destructive behavior.

Much of the misunderstanding exists because early writers did not have the appropriate language tools that were adequate to interpret psychological principles. Today, we know about the influence of the subconscious.

They didn't! Today, we understand some of the processes of the brain. They didn't! Today, we realize there are connections between emotional sensations, mental expectations, and physical phenomena. They didn't!

The importance of the Holy Spirit event on the day of Pentecost lies in its practical, personal application. God may be an abstract, ideological concept; Jesus may be a concrete, historical person; but the Holy Spirit can be an intimate psychological reality.

When we have emotional assurance and confidence, when we sense the moral guidance of our conscience, when we live by our intellectual insights and values, when we are forgiving and tolerant in social relationships, and when we use our creative abilities to the fullest, we are experiencing and utilizing the Holy Spirit. How much our actual thoughts and deeds are affected, however, depends upon our own willingness to listen carefully and respond wisely.

Throughout our lives heavenly signals are coming to us. Throughout our lives divine messages are being sent. Throughout our lives admonitions and directions are being given. The reason we don't receive them may be because we aren't tuned in. We may not have learned the spiritual language, or we may simply be refusing to follow the advice.

One of the clearest and most important scriptural concepts is that the Holy Spirit is within us. Paul says, "Do you not know that your body is a temple of the Holy Spirit within you, which you have from God?" (1 Cor 6:19).

The Holy Spirit lifts us above our natural selfish instincts. Paul says, "You are not in the flesh; you are in the Spirit, since the Spirit of God dwells in you" (Rom 8:9).

The Holy Spirit helps us recognize truth and inspires us to live productively. Jesus says, "If you love me, you will keep my commandments. And I will ask the Father, and he will give you another Advocate, to be with you forever. This is the Spirit of truth, whom the world cannot receive because it neither sees him nor knows him. You know him because he abides with you, and he will be in you" (John 14:15–17).

The Holy Spirit strengthens our will and gives us courage. Paul says, "I pray that, according to the riches of his glory, he may grant that you may be strengthened in your inner being with power through his Spirit" (Eph 3:16).

The Holy Spirit is not only in us; the Holy Spirit is an intrinsic part of us. This Spirit enhances our physical senses and affects what we see and hear and say and do. This empowers us to be the best we can be.

It's evident that few of us live up to our full potential. Most of us use only a fraction of the abilities we possess. Psychologists say the average person operates at about a twenty percent level of efficiency. That's shocking! Imagine a football team that had eleven men but only sent in two to play the game. Imagine a football coach who took nine men off the field and left just a center and a quarterback. Imagine any athletic group operating at twenty-percent efficiency. They would never win!

Neither can we! To conquer life we need to operate at peak efficiency. The Holy Spirit helps us do that.

Researchers tell about a strength test in which people were asked to grip a dynamometer as hard as they could. After the first squeeze had been measured, they were hypnotized and told they were very strong. Now, when asked to grip the device, their scores were better. But when they were hypnotized again and told they were very weak, their scores dropped dramatically.

Of course, our actual physical strength can't be increased or decreased by hypnosis, but our ability to use that strength can be affected. When we believe we are stronger or weaker, we react accordingly. There is a sense in which we all go through life hypnotized. Much of what we do is determined by what others have told us we can do and by what we tell ourselves. If this information is negative and false, that diminishes us. The Holy Spirit can help us overcome these obstacles.

No subject is more relevant than the Holy Spirit. The Holy Spirit is Christianity personalized. The Holy Spirit is religion individualized. Each of us reflects a facet of God that no one else can reflect. Each of us is able to achieve kingdom purposes that no one else can achieve.

One essential function of the Holy Spirit is to give assurance. Paul explained that, saying, "[God] has put his seal on us and given us his Spirit in our hearts as a down payment" (2 Cor 1:22). Since God knows a sense of security is essential to our well-being, he gives us an unconditional guarantee. The Holy Spirit is the tangible proof of our divine inheritance. When we have a sense of self-worth, when we have inner peace, and when we feel God's presence, that's the work of the Holy Spirit.

Authenticity is also crucial for health and happiness. God detests hypocrisy. John says, "If we say that we have fellowship with him while we are walking in darkness, we lie and do not do what is true" (1 John 1:6). In other words, if our lips don't match our lives, we're deceiving ourselves and others.

Paul associated this type of deceit with the destruction of the conscience. He criticized the deceit and called it "the hypocrisy of liars whose consciences are seared with a hot iron" (1Tim 4:2). A seared conscience has a tough, scarred overlay. It has lost its sensitivity. It isn't able to feel anymore. In short, it's worthless! Damage to the conscience or destruction of the conscience is dangerous because the Holy Spirit works through our conscience.

Human beings are almost infinitely adaptable. This is a survival skill, and it's essential to life, but it can also be destructive. Over time, negative conditioning can destroy our conscience. This deactivates our moral warning system and lulls us into a false sense of security.

Smoke alarms with dead batteries are worse than no smoke alarms at all. They are worse because we have been taught to depend on them. Since we expect them to warn us, we are less alert to other clues. Likewise, a conscience that has been perverted can be worse than not having a conscience at all. It's worse because we have been taught to depend on it. Since we expect the conscience to warn us, we are less alert to other clues. "Let your conscience be your guide" is a universal motto, but it's only as valid as the health and sensitivity of the conscience.

If we use empty excuses to justify a decision, if we pretend to agree when we don't, if we push undesirable feelings down into our subconscious, if we claim to believe things we know to be false, we're perverting our conscience and deceiving the Holy Spirit. If we continue doing this, we'll lose our ability to discriminate. Then we'll actually think we're being honest even when we're lying. Once this happens, we're helpless. That's why this sin is fatal.

Biologists tell of an experiment with frogs. They say when they drop a frog into a pan of hot water, it immediately realizes the danger and hops out with little harm done. However, if they put a frog in a pan of tepid water and then gradually increase the temperature, the frog will sit there until it dies, never realizing that the water is getting too hot. That's conditioning!

The reason certain respectable sins do so much damage is because we deny we're committing them. Rationalizing selfish actions and justifying cowardly behavior are dangerous habits. Sometimes, however, we must make conscious situational decisions that are not perfect. Life doesn't always give us absolutely right or absolutely wrong choices. Instead, there are occasions when we must pick the lesser of two evils. But if we are aware of this, realize the reasons for the problem, and admit the fault, this won't destroy our conscience. In other words, sins we recognize and confess are not as destructive as sins we hide and deny.

To stay honest and authentic amid propaganda and misleading public opinion, we need a reliable moral guide. Jesus said that's one essential function of the Holy Spirit: "When the Spirit of truth comes, he will guide you into all the truth" (John 16:13).

Many religions present their followers with a list of rules and say, "The way is marked! Follow these directions." If you're lost in the wilderness, however, having a globe or a world map isn't very helpful. Jesus knew this, so he sent the Holy Spirit to act as our personal guide.

In this road trip called life, we cannot see around the curve into tomorrow or over the hill into next week. Consequently, we can't avoid any obstacles, barriers, or dangers that may be ahead, and we're never sure when it's safe to pass. An omniscient God who sees the end from the beginning does know and wants to guide us. That's the great advantage of having God within instead of trying to follow written instructions or remember oral commandments. An internal truth detector allows us to operate boldly and naturally.

When we stay in touch with our guide, we can avoid pitfalls. When we follow our highest instincts, when we avoid tempting shortcuts, when we feel right about our choices, when we keep our conscience sensitive and our moral warning apparatus intact, that's the work of the Holy Spirit. An honest conscience allows us to become self-disciplined and independent. It enables us to make decisions and adjust as necessary to stay on the best course.

In a complicated world that offers a multitude of options, we need guidance. Certain airplanes have a radio beam that operates with auditory beeps. When the plane is directly on the beam, the pilot hears a constant hum. But when the plane veers off course, he hears a warning signal. In this way the jet is guided unerringly to its destination. This represents a wonderful triumph of inventive genius, but there's something within us that is even more wonderful than a radio beam. It's that divine beam of truth and light called the conscience. To follow that guide is to follow the Holy Spirit.

False ideas can cause a lot of damage. Don't lie to yourself. Don't set up invalid belief systems. Don't rely on illusions. Don't rationalize your selfish actions. Don't justify your destructive behaviors. Above all, don't reject truth.

Once, religious leaders refused to look through Galileo's telescope because they were afraid they might see astronomical evidence that would refute their doctrines. Today, members of a congregation may see discrepancies between life in the real world and the teachings of their church, but they just "don't think about it." Students may refuse to read certain books by agnostic scientists because they fear they'll be contaminated or persuaded.

People tend to resist new ideas because they are hard to assimilate. Suppose you are traveling and get all your bags packed for the flight home. Everything fits nicely. The latches are closed, the straps are fastened, and the locks are secure. Then you find a forgotten souvenir in a drawer or under the bed. Suppose this stray basket or carving or gadget is awkward and oddly shaped. Suppose, in order to put it in your luggage, you would have to unlock the lock, unfasten the straps, undo the latches, and move everything around to accommodate it. Wouldn't you be tempted to throw it in the trash?

We face this same situation when we're confronted with a new fact or a disturbing discovery that contradicts our current beliefs. We are tempted to forget it, deny it, or discard it rather than rearrange our entire value system. The decision is even harder if including this object or idea would force us to get rid of current possessions that give us comfort. In that case, it's much easier to ignore it.

But ignoring messages from the Holy Spirit leads to other problems. "I won't see" soon turns into "I can't see!" "I won't hear" soon turns into "I can't hear!" "I won't think" soon turns into "I can't think!" "I won't admit" soon turns into "I can't admit!" "I won't change" soon turns into "I can't change!" That's why when facts or discoveries contradict the opinions or values or beliefs we already hold, it's tempting to say, "I see no conflict! I hear no conflict! There is no conflict!" Such a mindset keeps us from assimilating useful information. It keeps us from accepting new ideas. It keeps us from progressing or maturing. Change is absolutely essential.

An eggshell provides a wonderful parable of doctrinal flexibility. It shows us we don't have to apologize for outgrowing certain beliefs. We don't have to feel guilty about changing our theological stance. A shell is a suitable covering for the chick embryo at a certain period of its existence, but it's totally unsuitable later. At some point that shell must be broken. Not because it is wrong or evil, but because change is right and good and inevitable!

In our fast-paced, technological world today, we are often required to make instantaneous decisions. It's fortunate that the Holy Spirit can even help us to make the right response in those moments of crisis. Jesus said, "The Holy Spirit will teach you at that very hour what you ought to say" (Luke 12:12).

As Christians, we need to realize the Holy Spirit uses our own mental faculties. It refreshes our memories and helps us recall past information. Jesus said, "The Advocate, the Holy Spirit, whom the Father will send in my name, will teach you everything and remind you of all that I have said to you" (John 14:26).

The Holy Spirit enables us to analyze deep ideas and examine profound concepts. Paul tells us, "God has revealed to us through the Spirit, for the Spirit searches everything, even the depths of God" (1 Cor 2:10).

The Holy Spirit also gives us conviction about sin. When we feel remorse, when we regret causing pain, when our conscience hurts, when we're sensitive to other people's burdens, that's the work of the Holy Spirit. When we have an urge to achieve a worthy goal, when we overcome inertia and apathy, when we exert extra effort to succeed in a good cause, when we persist in the face of obstacles, when we develop and use our abilities and talents, that's the work of the Holy Spirit.

Having the Holy Spirit within increases our security and authenticity. It causes our subconscious to respond accurately and automatically. It allows us to trust our intuition. Having the Holy Spirit within enables us to have a healthy balance between the emotional, moral, mental, social, and physical areas of life.

God's divine presence in our lives can give us the ability to understand scriptures concerning sins against the Holy Spirit. This subject has created much unnecessary anxiety. We know that an intelligent, loving God wouldn't decree one crucial, mysterious commandment that can be accidently broken and never forgiven. We know that an intelligent, loving God wouldn't establish one fatal offense that can be committed through ignorance and thereby doom us to eternal punishment.

In fact, the scriptures mention five kinds of transgressions against the Holy Spirit. The first sin is to blaspheme: "Whoever blasphemes against the Holy Spirit can never have forgiveness but is guilty of an eternal sin" (Mark 3:29; see also Matt 12:31; Luke 12:10). This statement is probably the most disturbing teaching in all the scriptures. It indicates that to revile, to speak evil of, to vilify, or to damage the Holy Spirit is the most serious transgression of humankind.

Why is this deed so deadly? It would seem there are worse offenses. Murder, child molestation, terrorism, and many other sins seem more destructive, so why did Jesus zero in on this particular sin? It may well be because this sin destroys that most precious thing known as self-worth.

This would also help to explain another strange admonition Jesus gave about the treatment of others: He warns us that "if you are angry with a brother or sister, you will be liable to judgment, and if you insult a brother or sister, you will be liable to the council, and if you say, 'You fool,' you will be liable to the hell of fire" (Matt 5:22).

Again, why on earth did Jesus get so vehement about mere terminology? Surely other things are more important! Yet that's what he said: "You are guilty!"

The word *raca*, which some Bible translations use, means worthless and empty. The word *fool* means dull or stupid. Such name-callings and verbal putdowns are serious sins. Words can hurt. Verbal abuse causes deep wounds. It attacks self-esteem and destroys feelings of self-worth. The victims of verbal abuse tend to become what they are labeled. Psychologists say children value themselves to the degree they have been valued. We believe the image of ourselves that others mirror back to us, even if that mirror is distorted.

Blaspheming the Holy Spirit is an unpardonable sin because the value of a soul is at stake!

The second sin is to deceive: "'Ananias,' Peter asked, 'why has Satan filled your heart to lie to the Holy Spirit, and to keep back part of the proceeds of the land?'" (Acts 5:3).

We lie to the Holy Spirit by practicing self-deception. If we rationalize, deny, suppress, and condition our conscience long enough, we'll no longer be able to recognize reality when we see it. If we fool ourselves once too often, we'll begin to believe the lies, and our moral apparatus will cease to operate!

A woman and her two children drowned in a lake. There were campers nearby who could have saved them, but they had become accustomed to hearing the children's playful shouts for help, so they ignored the cries when they were real. They said the children had been yelling all day, so people didn't believe them anymore. Lives could have been saved if bystanders had taken the children's screams seriously. Practicing deceit, even in minor matters, is a dangerous thing.

As important as it is to be able to trust others, it's vastly more important to be able to trust ourselves! If we squelch our true feelings and refuse to admit our true beliefs, we are practicing internal deceit. Eventually, we won't be able to get in touch with our true feelings and our true beliefs. We'll be alienated from our own inner being, and that's fatal. As long as we excuse our sins and deny our weaknesses, we can't grow. As long as we blame our failures on circumstances or on other people, we can't change.

Moral guidelines are essential elements of life. If we excuse ourselves and silence this inner voice, we're deceiving the Holy Spirit.

The third sin is to resist. Stephen criticized stubborn individuals, saying, "You stiff-necked people, uncircumcised in heart and ears, you are forever opposing the Holy Spirit" (Acts 7:51).

When we are confronted with truth and refuse to acknowledge it, we're resisting the Holy Spirit. When we have an opportunity to learn and do not take advantage of it, we're resisting the Holy Spirit.

Our modern word for this condition is *mindset*. Once our outlook or opinion gets set into concrete, no growth can occur. Once our outlook or opinion gets stuck in a rut, no harmonious relationships can be achieved.

Intellectual challenge is essential to a healthy life. Resisting the Holy Spirit over a period of time dulls our mental faculties and takes away our free will.

The fourth sin is to grieve. Paul says, "Do not grieve the Holy Spirit of God, with which you were marked with a seal for the day of redemption. Put away from you all bitterness and wrath and anger and wrangling and slander, together with all malice" (Eph 4:30–31).

This word *grieve* means to cause distress. He says we grieve and distress the Holy Spirit when we are unforgiving, angry, contentious, and hateful. Instead, we must "be kind to one another, tenderhearted, forgiving one another, just as God in Christ also has forgiven you" (Eph 4:32).

Medical and psychological authorities now know that negative emotions, such as resentment and hatred, do cause great distress! They hurt our bodies and twist our minds. Social sensitivity and productive interaction are also essential elements of life. A pattern of either isolation or confrontation between people grieves the Holy Spirit.

The fifth sin is to quench. Paul said, "Do not quench the Spirit" (1 Thess 5:19).

This word *quench* literally means to extinguish. We do this when we fail to develop our potential and when we neglect service to others. You quench or extinguish a candle flame by snuffing it out or by cutting off its supply of oxygen. Paul indicates that the Holy Spirit can likewise be diminished or extinguished by cutting off our supply of knowledge and information or by doing things that harm our bodies, damage our minds, or lower our self-respect.

Lack of self-worth leads to other problems. A recent study found one commonality among criminals, alcoholics, drug addicts, and patients with severe mental illnesses: low self-esteem. Low self-worth sets up a vicious cycle. We begin to believe "If I'm not worth much, then I can't do much. Therefore, I don't do much. Thus, I soon have more concrete evidence that I'm not worth much."

Instead, we should show reverence for the God who is within us. We should correctly evaluate and appreciate ourselves and our abilities. We should develop an optimistic and confident outlook on life. We should exemplify a permanent attitude of personal self-assurance.

It's terrible to have to "quench the spirit" to survive. It's terrible to have to cover up our talents and camouflage our personalities to be accepted. Girls who let boys beat them at sports to be popular are "quenching the spirit." Men who submit to egotistical bosses to get promotions are "quenching the spirit." Politicians who vote in dishonest ways to ensure reelection are "quenching the spirit." Christians who agree to false orthodoxy to avoid reprimands are "quenching the spirit."

Quenching the Spirit is fatal because it kills the unique essence of a human being. It keeps us from developing and maturing. Just as one numeral is essential and valuable in mathematics and one letter is essential and valuable in the alphabet, one soul is essential and valuable in God's kingdom. Each creation needs to be protected, nourished, and honored, not quenched.

Self-imposed attitudes hold us back as effectively as physical circumstances. Denying our abilities, neglecting our talents, and refusing to exercise our intellect is immoral. A mind and a soul and a life are too important to waste. Quenching the Holy Spirit is deadly because God's kingdom depends upon us! Quenching the Holy Spirit is deadly because each person is unique. Each person is a one-of-a-kind original! Each person is essential and valuable. Since my viewpoint is different from everyone else's, I must reflect my particular facet to its fullest.

A salesman told a lady buying a rechargeable hand vacuum, "Don't use it just a little. Instead, run it completely down each time. The reason is simple. This device only recharges to the level of ordinary use. If it gets adjusted to expecting a small energy depletion, then it will only recharge to accommodate that amount." That's also true of us! We tend to gradually reduce our productivity to the level of ordinary output. So using only a fraction of our potential is quenching the Holy Spirit.

Now, let's summarize the sins against the Holy Spirit: When we show a lack of respect for the God within, when we put ourselves down and lower our self-esteem, we are blaspheming the Holy Spirit. When we try to rationalize our conscience and deny our senses, we are deceiving the Holy Spirit. When we refuse to acknowledge and follow truth, we are resisting the Holy Spirit. When we have hateful, destructive attitudes and perpetrate hurtful, non-productive deeds, we are grieving the Holy Spirit. When we extinguish or diminish our talents and refuse to live up to our potential, we are quenching the Holy Spirit. All these sins are fatal because all of them cut us off from our life source. They clog the pipeline through which we receive divine revelation and spiritual guidance.

We must understand that the unpardonable sin is not something we commit by making one wrong decision. It's seldom the momentous events that determine our destiny. Instead, it's the simple, everyday acts practiced over a long period of time. Seemingly insignificant choices shape our habits. Then those habits mold our character, and our character determines our fate. The unpardonable sin means that a soul has gone past the ethical point of no return!

Some transoceanic planes are equipped with an operational instrument that ensures perfect flying conditions, correct mechanical processes, and expert handling. It's there to help the captain evaluate his progress by comparing the actual flight with the ideal one. The pilot has many opportunities to change his mind and return to the terminal. However, at one place on the chart, a line is drawn. This is called the "point of no return." Once a pilot has passed that point, he must proceed. He no longer has options. He is now committed to his course.

Life is like that. If we don't respect the God within, if we doubt our self-worth, if we rationalize our conscience, if we deny our senses, if we refuse to acknowledge and follow truth, if we have hateful attitudes and perpetuate hurtful deeds, if we extinguish our talents and refuse to live up to our potential, we will eventually pass the "point of no return." That's fatal!

The reason these sins cannot be forgiven is because they are self-inflicted. Individuals who commit them are destroying their own spiritual guidance system. They have chosen to eliminate their personal connection to God. They have cut off all access to a merciful heavenly Father. That's why they are called "unpardonable sins."

Jesus said, "When the Spirit of truth comes, he will guide you into all the truth" (John 16:13). The scriptures also assure us that we are made in God's image and are commanded to have dominion here on earth (see Gen 1:26–28). This means God has given human beings a lot of responsibility. We may not realize this because many religions have taught that a sovereign God is in complete control, and as his subjects, we're to just be obedient, submissive slaves.

This is not, and has never been, a scriptural truth or even a reasonable truth. It's obvious to any sane person that we as human beings have been put in charge of earthly affairs. God doesn't build houses or plant corn or invent space capsules. We do! God doesn't fix our mistakes or mend our broken appliances. We do!

The psalmist said, "The heavens are the LORD's heavens, but the earth he has given to human beings" (Ps 115:16). This doesn't mean, however, that he has left us alone and helpless! On the contrary, he gave us a complex body that can often heal itself. He gave us an awesome brain that adapts to circumstances and develops innovations that improve life. He provides every resource we need to survive and thrive. Surely such a creator is not just sitting there on a throne in heaven hoping to get praise, adoration, and obeisance from groups of mortals. Instead, God is involved in our lives and concerned about his kingdom here on earth. Through the Holy Spirit within, he is constantly sending insights, urges, and aspirations to all individuals who are willing to be his children, heirs, and agents.

God calls us to serve. He enables us to succeed, and he advises us how to choose wisely. If the creator made us in his image and according to his likeness, let's act for him! If the creator gave us the authority to take dominion over all earthly affairs, let's do our job!

It's fortunate we can know and relate to God by developing our own personal intuition and insights.

Conclusion

Many theologians use these three attributes to describe God: omniscience, omnipotence, and omnipresence. If omniscience is to know all, then to know nothing or to be ignorant is its opposite, and therefore a sin. If omnipotence is to be able to do all, then to be able to do nothing or to be weak and passive is its opposite, and therefore a sin. If omnipresence is to be in all places, then to be in no place, or to have a narrow existence, is its opposite, and therefore a sin.

These logical analogies of God's attributes indicate that the more we know and understand, the closer we are to godlikeness. The more we exercise self-control and take charge of our lives, the closer we are to godlikeness. The broader our vision and the wider our horizons, the closer we are to godlikeness.

Knowledge is all around us. It exists everywhere. It has existed since the beginning of time and will continue to exist until the end of time. But too often we're unaware of it. Electricity would have served Abraham if he had only known how to develop and use it.

God wants us to know. If he didn't expect us to exercise independence and use our abilities, he wouldn't have made us managers over creation. The greatest mistake most religions have made is to encourage their members to be gullible and subservient. God wants us to be more than slaves, more than servants, and more than subjects. He wants us to be sons and daughters.

Once, a new guard at a monarch's palace gate stopped a young man and rudely snapped, "Subjects of the realm are not allowed beyond this point."

"You don't understand," the youth replied. "I'm more than a subject. I'm a son!"

God has ordained us to be the potential rulers of the universe. Jesus said, "To the one who conquers I will give a place with me on my throne, just as I myself conquered and sat down with my Father on his throne" (Rev 3:21).

God is a wise creator. Evil is self-destructing, and good is self-perpetuating. This principle is built into the moral system to assure progress and ultimate victory. Evil may enjoy temporary triumphs, but it will experience permanent defeat. In casinos or gambling establishments, the odds are preset so that even though in specific instances the house or machine may lose to a gambler, over the long term the house and machines are assured of winning.

Life is like that. Over the long term, circumstances are preset to guarantee us that truth will triumph over falsehood, goodness will defeat evil, and right will win over wrong. Jesus said, "Take courage: I have conquered the world!" (John 16:33).

Although the effects of evil are very real, evil itself can't live on its own. In most cases it's merely a perversion of good. It defiles the emotions, distorts the will, and invades the soul. That's why Jesus said truth would make us free (see John 8:32). He clearly stated his overall purpose when he said, "For this I was born, and for this I came into the world, to testify to the truth" (John 18:37).

The psalmists also emphasize truth, saying, "O send out your light and your truth; let them lead me" (Ps 43:3).

David said, "You desire truth in the inward being" (Ps 51:6).

Solomon said, "Buy truth, and do not sell it" (Prov 23:23).

The power of truth is weakened when we neglect or abuse it. Truth is perverted when we use slant and innuendo or arrange facts to give false impressions. In vicious political propaganda the material is slanted. In unethical advertising the statements are slanted. In malicious gossip the information is slanted. Ulterior motives cause us to twist and misuse truth, and a half-truth can be worse than a lie.

Once, a stern ship captain hauled in a young officer and reprimanded him for a wild night on shore. "I've never done this before, sir, and I'll never do it again," pleaded the boy. "If you put this in the record, it will ruin my career. Please give me another chance."

"I have no tolerance," raved the captain. "We record the exact truth in this log." And he wrote, "The first mate was drunk today."

A few weeks later, this first mate was left in charge of the ship's log, and he wrote, "The captain was sober today."

When the intolerant captain read it, he was furious and shouted, "This statement makes it sound as if my being sober is unusual. It insinuates that I'm often drunk. Delete this innuendo at once!"

"Oh, no, sir," replied the first mate, "we write the exact truth in this log."

Truth is a valuable commodity, and it must be handled with care. It must not be used for selfish purposes. Hate can masquerade as righteous indignation. Pride can masquerade as personal esteem. Revenge can masquerade as legal justice.

Evil has to impersonate good to survive. It has to insert legitimate words into misleading statements to give them credibility. It's dangerous to tamper with truth.

God has given us a beautiful earth and an awe-inspiring universe. His creative possibilities are infinite. An acorn can become a forest. A grain of wheat can become enough bread to feed the world. One microscopic cell can become an elephant. A baby can become a Christ.

An observation of nature assures us that life is invincible. Whether it's a grass blade penetrating concrete or a young genius triumphing over a difficult upbringing, life is empowered by God.

It's our responsibility to care for the resources and overcome the obstacles. The only difference between a winner and a loser is that the winner gets up after he falls. Peter and Judas both denied and betrayed their Lord. Peter got up. Judas didn't.

For Christians, despair is not an option. There is always hope. Jesus said, "The one who endures to the end will be saved" (Matt 10:22).

One of the final promises in the Bible says, "Be faithful until death, and I will give you the crown of life" (Rev 2:10).

God also expects unity and agreement. He knows that "a house divided cannot stand." It takes everyone working together to bring in the kingdom. If children sitting around a jigsaw puzzle each grab a handful of pieces and try to construct separate pictures, they will all fail. Instead, each child must share pieces with the group. Everyone must cooperate before a complete picture can emerge.

That's also true in life. Diverse workers, such as scientists, theologians, educators, and farmers, must all contribute their unique insights, experiences, and achievements before some projects can be completed.

Life itself has unity. If you fly over a group of islands and look down, they appear to be individual spots of land irrevocably separated by water. If you could dive deep enough, however, you'd find that they are all solidly connected to the geological unit.

Likewise, there are areas of life that seem to be completely unrelated. If you go deep enough, however, you'll find that they are solidly connected. Paul says the arms and legs and ears and eyes must all work together for the physical body (see 1 Cor 12:12–25).

Christians seem to forget that God created this wonderful world. Too often we've separated religion from life. We've pitted the heart against the brain. We've emphasized feelings and denigrated thinking. We've condemned the secular elements and praised the sacred elements. That's a tragic mistake because Jesus presented spirituality as a vital part of life. He said, "I came that they might have life and have it abundantly" (John 10:10).

Jesus never indicated we must choose between our faith and science, between our faith and reason, or between our faith and common sense. Instead, he knew faith motivates science, faith utilizes reason, and faith is the very basis of common sense. James said, "Faith by itself, if it has no works, is dead" (Jas 2:17).

In God's world, the many disciplines and areas of knowledge all work together for the cosmic body. Certain medical cures cannot be developed, certain astronomical achievements cannot be realized, and certain mechanical breakthroughs cannot be accomplished until the connections are made. We don't need more specialists. Instead, we need more synthesizers.

The church must equip and encourage its members to be connectors. Often, we hear a stirring sermon urging us to "take up our cross." We leave the church service with good intentions, determined to try. But how? It sounds so irrelevant. We might read an extra chapter in the Bible on Sunday night, but when the alarm clock goes off on Monday morning, we're immediately involved in packing lunches, working with relationship problems, and running errands. These activities are seemingly far removed from cross-bearing."

A theology that exhorts us to "do God's will" doesn't seem to be related to frying potatoes and passing history tests. That's why well-meaning, sensitive people often begin to live with feelings of slight discomfort. This discomfort is followed by guilt and confusion. Gradually, they begin to compartmentalize. To cope they develop this motto: "Life must be life, and religion must be religion, and never the twain shall meet!" This problem must be solved for our faith to affect our daily behavior.

Jesus constantly dealt with this issue. Sacrificial systems, priestly rituals, and irrelevant rules had become so totally separated from daily life that they were a farce—a hypocritical routine, a deadly duty. Jesus even dared to ridicule the orthodox practices of his day. He scoffed at their long prayers, wide phylacteries, ceremonial cleansings, fasts, and Sabbath-day regulations. Now, remember, these doctrines and practices were well-entrenched dogmas. They were as important to those people as our religious doctrines and traditions are to us.

Both theologians and laymen who do religious research have discovered it's hard to synchronize the secular and spiritual worlds. Admiral Byrd, the first man to fly over the South Pole, told of a rather strange experience he had when he and his crew were flying parallel to the international date line. He said, "On one side of this imaginary boundary it was Tuesday, but if we moved over just a few feet to the other side, it was Wednesday. Strong winds and inadequate equipment caused us to keep zig-zagging from today into tomorrow and then back again."

As Christians in this world, we occupy a similar position. Our lives parallel the boundaries of the physical and spiritual dimensions. We live in the reality of today, yet we must be able to cross over into the idealism of tomorrow. Since we are representatives of God, we cannot afford to remain ignorant. We cannot afford to be negligent. We cannot afford to worship an unknown God.

Worshiping a God we don't know is dangerous because everyone tends to emulate the character and behavior of their object of worship. If we have false assumptions or negative notions about God, this will affect our own moral development.

Any deceitful, vengeful, or unproductive traits that we assign to God will eventually be incorporated into our own lives. Then they will be acted out in harmful ways on the people around us. That's why our "search for God" must be serious and successful. He has promised that if we seek him with all our heart, we will find him (see Jer 29:13).

Now, let's summarize our five paths to knowledge: First, the scriptures say, "The heavens are telling the glory of God, and the firmament proclaims his handiwork" (Ps 19:1). So let's discover all we can from nature itself. As we appreciate our world's awesome grandeur and admire its many beautiful features, we must conclude that God is both intelligent and aesthetic.

Next, Jesus said, "Whoever has seen me has seen the Father" (John 14:9). So let's study Jesus's message and ministry to get information about him. As we observe his acts of common sense and mercy, we must conclude that God is impartial and accepting.

Then, Solomon said, "From [God's] mouth come[s] knowledge" (Prov 2:6). So let's research the insights and revelations of scriptural prophets and theologians to find out what they discovered. As we learn from these dedicated thinkers, we must conclude God is righteous and consistent.

Jesus told us to "have love for one another" (John 13:35). So let's notice and appreciate the many good deeds and unselfish acts of the people around us. As we develop relationships with caring men and women, we must conclude God is compassionate and generous.

Finally, Jesus wants us to use our own personal intuition and insight. He said, "The Holy Spirit…will teach you everything" (John 14:26). So let's learn how to recognize the still small voice of the Holy Spirit. As we listen and respond to spiritual counsel, we must conclude God calls us to serve, enables us to succeed, and advises us how to choose wisely.

So do you really know the God you worship? Informed Christian disciples must be able to answer these questions: Can you recommend your God's character as a moral model? Can you proudly describe your God's ethical principles to non-believers? Can you use your God's purposes as your own standards and ideals?

God wants us to know him. He promises that in the future everyone will know him. The Lord says, "I will put my laws in their minds and write them on their hearts, and I will be their God, and they shall be my people. And they shall not teach one another or say to each other, 'Know the Lord,' for they shall all know me, from the least of them to the greatest" (Heb 8:10–11).

www.ingramcontent.com/pod-product-compliance
Lightning Source LLC
Chambersburg PA
CBHW071011160426
43193CB00012B/2005